CU00802247

This book shoul
Lancashire Coun:

BARN...SW...r
s/09
0128...1214...
2 7 JUL 2009
2 8 AUG 2009

3A
the
...ore the date shown

That's
who
D'is'in

1 3 OCT 2014

2 1 DEC 2012   2 7 NOV 2014

1 1 JUL 2013 — **9 JAN 2015**

2 2 AUG 2013   **2 8 APR 2015**

Third Age Press

ISBN 1 898576 23 8
First edition

Third Age Press Ltd, 2008
Third Age Press, 6 Parkside Gardens
London SW19 5EY
Managing Editor Dianne Norton

Front cover photo from *Illustrated* September 15 1956

Photographs and playbills
from the Patrick Newley collection

Cover & layout design by Dianne Norton
Printed and bound in Great Britain
by IntypeLibra London

YOU LUCKY PEOPLE!

THE TOMMY TRINDER STORY

by

PATRICK NEWLEY

ABOUT THE AUTHOR

PATRICK NEWLEY is a longstanding contributor
to both *The Times* and *The Stage* newspapers. He has
also written for *The Daily Express* and many other
publications. A frequent broadcaster for the BBC,
he was press agent for the writers Quentin Crisp and
Robin Maugham. He managed the later careers of
both the legendary revue artiste Douglas Byng and
the comedian Rex Jameson (Mrs Shufflewick).
He lives in London.

FOR CHUBBY OATES

Stand-up comedy? You walk out there and you have to prove to the audience that irrespective of what they think or whatever happens, you're the guv'nor.

(Tommy Trinder)

CONTENTS

ILLUSTRATIONS

INTRODUCTION

Tommy Trinder was one of Britain's greatest comics; an egotistical, aggressive, working-class performer who was regarded by many as the greatest ad-libber in showbusiness. His catchphrases, 'You lucky people!' and 'If it's laughter you're after, Trinder's the name!' became famous nationwide and his act, filled with insult and sexual innuendo, was rarely scripted. 'Trinder was a personality,' said the comedian Max Wall. 'He was himself. He was incorrigible. There was only one TT.'

Although he was himself a product of the music hall, the roots of modern British stand-up comedy – honed in recent years by the likes of Billy Connolly, Jasper Carrot, Peter Kay and Jack Dee – can be directly traced back to Trinder's unique performing style. He set the fashion for the unrehearsed ad-lib and grinned disdainfully at authority. He insulted his audiences and they adored him for it. Roy Hudd observed that Trinder was an 'alternative' comic before the phrase had ever been thought of.

He was a pioneer of live television stand-up comedy and, at the height of his fame during the 1940s and 50s, enjoyed superstar status, a rarity for any comedian then or since. He understood the power of celebrity and manipulated the media. Rarely a day went by when he wasn't in the news.

On stage and off he was a monstrous egotist, a walking self-advertisment who, like entertainers such as Al Jolson and Noel Coward, was incandescent with belief in himself. And, like Ethel Merman, he adhered to the maxim, 'When I do a show, the whole show revolves around me.'

Egotism is a common trait with great talent but it was not always popular with Trinder's fellow performers. Whilst comics such as Arthur Askey, Max Wall and Barry Humphries revered him, the likes of Bruce Forsyth and musical comedy stars such as Pat Kirkwood and Evelyn Laye did not. 'There was a cruel streak to Trinder as a performer,' said Pat Kirkwood. 'Many a co-star came a cropper with him. He had to be number one all the time.'

Yet few British comics' careers have been so varied and few performers have been held in such affection by the public as Trinder. From performing as a boy in music halls, to topping the London Palladium more times than any other comic, he was also a top box office film star. During World War Two no artiste worked harder or in more hazardous conditions than he did, entertaining civilians and troops alike at the height of the Blitz as well as touring in ENSA shows throughout Europe, North Africa and the Far East.

His private life was equally colourful. A heavy smoker but a lifelong teetotaller – an oddity for a comedian – he was a keen sports fan and a longtime chairman of Fulham Football Club. He loved jazz music, bought cars, owned a yacht, gave thousands of pounds to charity and often discreetly helped many fellow performers in need.

He was also a notorious, high-spending womaniser and loved the company of beautiful girls – whether they had a husband or not. He was flash, well groomed and highly sexed.

'I co-starred with him at the London Palladium in the forties revue *Happy and Glorious,*' said musical comedy star Sheila Mathews. 'I had the dressing room next door to him and every night you could hear the bonking going on. It was so loud the walls would shudder.'

Twice married, his long suffering first wife, Vi, divorced him because of his infidelity although he later found stability and happiness with his second wife, Tonie.

I first came across Tommy Trinder when I was growing up in the 1960s. I had a penchant for film comedy – especially Americans like the Marx Brothers and Bob Hope – and I devoured TV programmes such as Bob Monkhouse's *Mad Movies* which featured flickering silent clips of comic greats Charlie Chaplin and Harold Lloyd. Occasionally I watched British film comedies starring George Formby, which were dire, but the standout vintage comedies for me, often shown on boring Sunday afternoons, were those starring Tommy Trinder: *Champagne Charlie*, *Fiddlers Three* and *Sailors Three* – they were genuinely funny and had stood the test of time, as they still do today.

I got hooked on the ski-slope chinned, wisecracking Trinder. I loved his nerve, his rotten jokes and the way he pricked pomposity. I wanted to know more about him – so I asked my parents.

My dad had served in the RAF in World War Two in North Africa and had seen Trinder in ENSA shows. 'The troops loved him,' he said. 'We thought of him as one of the boys. He was jack-the-lad and he got massive laughs when he took the mickey out of the sergeant major or joked about the lousy food we had. He said all the things the ordinary soldier would have loved to have said.'

My mother was in the Wrens during the war. 'When we were on leave a crowd of us girls would often go to the Palladium to see Trinder,' she said. 'He was terribly funny and we all thought he was lovely. He was sexy, which is not the sort of word you would associate with a comedian. But he was definitely not the type you could ever take home to meet your parents. He looked much too naughty for that.'

Funny, bold, cheeky, sexy – even dangerous. That was Trinder.

I first saw him working live in 1973 when, as an 18-year-old actor, I was appearing in repertory at Butlins at Barry Island in South Wales. Every Sunday night there was a star variety show at the holiday camp's vast Gaiety Theatre,

although the top of the bill was always a surprise act. One Sunday the compère came on stage and told the audience that the star guest was 'a true show-biz legend.' The orchestra struck up the tune *Tiger Rag* and without

You Lucky People!

further announcement on bounced Tommy Trinder. There was a gasp of recognition from the audience and a huge round of applause. 'Yes, it's me,' boasted Trinder. 'You lucky people!'

He was then a chirpy, gravel-voiced 64-year-old and his gags, or rather quips, were amazingly topical, many of them culled from news items in that Sunday's papers. He didn't care what he said and even made jokes about the IRA who were then engaged in a fierce bombing campaign against Britain. It was dangerous comedy and the audience couldn't get enough of him.

Many veteran comics of Trinder's ilk played Butlins variety theatres in the sixties and seventies simply because they knew they had a guaranteed audience. Butlins audiences came to see the shows irrespective of who was on the bill. By the seventies Trinder's long career was on the wane and, although he rarely stopped working, he no longer commanded large fees or top billing and in many cases he was reduced to playing small parts in provincial pantomimes. Younger performers had little idea of his status as a comic and his audiences were usually made up of elderly fans.

Why should this be? For long periods in the fifties and sixties Trinder had worked abroad in Australia which meant he was an unfamiliar face to younger British audiences. He also had a longtime reputation for being difficult to work with. Even as late as 1980 he was fired, while in rehearsals, from a proposed touring production of *Pygmalion*, in which he was to have played Alfred Doolittle opposite Evelyn Laye's Mrs Higgins, because he wanted to ad-lib, although there is something rather endearing about the idea of him trying to improve Bernard Shaw's dialogue.

And, as he got older, he was rarely seen on television. He also chose not to write an autobiography, once flippantly claiming that the sight of a pile of unsold Ted Ray biographies in WH Smith's had put him off.

Yet he still commanded great respect from his fellow comics, who referred to him as 'the guv'nor', and his audiences, however small, were always loyal. The secret of his enduring appeal was undoubtedly his modernity. He moved with the times and his patter was always razor sharp.

For me, Trinder was the closest performer we had in Britain comparable to Groucho Marx. Like Groucho his humour was refreshingly free from pathos and he never asked for sympathy. The audience had to accept him on his own terms. And, like Groucho, he was always 'on' for any kind of performance or public appearance, ranging from a London Palladium show to lunch with a few relative strangers. He was the king of ad-lib and did not disappoint.

In any account of Trinder's life his name must always be synonymous with the London Palladium and it is surely fitting that his very last public appearance should have been at the world famous variety theatre just a few months before he died.

Tommy Trinder was a born raconteur and throughout his career could never resist reminiscing with journalists about his past. He also wrote many newspaper articles about his career and it is from these, notably *Illustrated Weekly* (1956), that I have taken various quotes for this memoir.The late Max Wall gave an in-depth and perceptive interview to Michael Pointon after Trinder's death and I am grateful to Michael for permission to quote from this.

TRINDER ON THE HALLS

'If it's laughter you're after, Trinder's the name!'

The key to Tommy Trinder's approach to performing on stage can be found in his early childhood. As a youngster he played boisterous games on the streets of South London and loved showing off. 'I was an extrovert,' he said. 'I always wanted to be the best. As a kid I played football and if I couldn't be captain I'd take the ball back.'

Although he was often described as a cockney comedian, his sharp witted, abrasive humour and gift for ad-libbing originated not from the East End but directly from those working class roots in Streatham, South London.

Trinder was born Thomas Edward Trinder at 54 Wellfield Road, just off the main High Road, Streatham, on March 24 1909, the son of Thomas Henry Trinder, a tram driver, and his wife Jean Mills. His brother Fred was the spitting image of him and was frequently mistaken for him during Trinder's career.

Most of the residents of Wellfield Road lived in cramped conditions. Their houses were overcrowded and amenities were scant. At one end of the road was a block of flats known as 'the incubator' because of the large families who lived there.

The Trinder family were not well off. Food was plentiful but cheap. Milk was tuppence a pint, potatoes seven pounds for three pence.

Trinder was just five when World War One broke out and on September 11 1914 Streatham saw its first enemy Zeppelin which passed harmlessly over the High Road to the sound of a boy scout blowing a bugle to warn residents of the danger of an air raid. Two years later on the night of September 24, Streatham was bombed in the German's sixth and most destructive raid on London. During a period of 15 minutes a Zeppelin had dropped a total of 32 bombs on Streatham. Seven people were killed and twenty seven seriously injured in what was the first night of destruction Streatham had ever known. Several bombs dropped directly on the High Road and others on the little villa roads to the right. Bomb holes were seen on the High Road and the walls of shops and houses were pitted with flying fragments of metal. Trinder and his mates eagerly searched for souvenirs of the raid, pieces of shattered glass were picked up and groups of youngsters paraded through the thoroughfare singing, *'Keep the home fires burning till the boys comes home.'*

The Trinder family moved to Fulham when Trinder's father was transferred to the Hammersmith tram depot. Tommy's formal education was minimal. He was briefly a pupil at St Andrew's School, Holborn but because the family were poor he left early and worked as an errand boy at Smithfield meat market.

At the age of 12 he entered a talent competition as a boy vocalist at Collins Music Hall in Islington. 'I had a voice like Deanna Durbin,' he recalled. He won first prize and got a job with Will Murray's *Casey's Court*, a survival of the Fred Karno style and forerunner to the Crazy Gang and toured with the company under the name of Red Nirt – his name spelt backwards.

'Will Murray arranged with my mother and father that I would get 7/6 a week and my keep. That was a godsend to my people as they couldn't get me packed off quick enough. 7/6 was the rent of the house. I opened at the Palace Theatre, Oldham, all clogs, shawls

Trinder as a boy

and cobblestones. My mother stitched a pound note into the lining of my jacket so that I would have the fare home if things went wrong. That jacket was ripped open before I got to Crewe. My job was to cut bread for the boys and we slept four in a bed. I was about 16 before I realised people slept longways.'

Dressed on stage in bright check trousers, bolero-style jacket and bowler hat, he went on to join an act called Phil Rees's Stable Lads and then worked the Folies Bergère in Paris for a year. On returning to London he began making solo appearances in working mens' clubs where he was paid 7/6d per night for singing three songs and eighteen pence extra for an encore. In between songs he began ad-libbing and telling jokes and, when eventually his voice broke, he dropped the songs and became a full time comic touring the lesser provincial halls.

As traditional music hall declined, variety flourished in the twenties and thirties when every major town had a variety theatre. In the north it had its roots firmly in the terraced streets and Lowry landscapes of the provinces and the theatres provided a cocoon of comfort and security that working class audiences were reluctant to leave. In the south there were dozens of variety theatres within a ten mile radius of the London Coliseum. 'If you ever wanted to know what London or Glasgow, Belfast, Leeds, Hull, Bristol or Manchester was really like,' said poet John Betjeman, 'you only had to go to the variety theatres to find out. There were the local jokes and there, very often, was the regional talent later to become famous throughout the country.'

Trinder was a London comic but unlike other southern comedians whose humour did not travel well, particularly in the north, he was equally at home in towns such as Middlesborough as he was in London. 'I worked with all the top variety acts and took the best laugh out of each of them. They were always the dirty ones. Every comic had one dirty gag that he used to punch them between the eyes with, so I had a right collection. I had the filthiest act in showbusiness and I wore more makeup than Grock. I had to look older to suit the type of material I was using.'

At the age of 17 he became a leading light with Archie Pitt's touring comedy shows, earning seven pounds a week. A seedy, short and balding figure, Pitt was an untalented cockney comedian but had great flair as a showman. In 1932 he became Gracie Fields' first husband.

Trinder spent years as a second turn on variety bills.'I played all the Moss Empires, second turn, twelve minutes,' he said. 'I stood in front of a backcloth covered with advertisements. It might depict a street scene. There would be an airship with McDougall's self-raising flour painted on the side; a box extolling the virtues of Ted's Night Powder; and an old man with a sandwich board urging you to eat in Barney's Cafe. The comic had to keep moving about the stage. If he stood in front of an advertisement for too long, the business which had bought the space would refuse to pay for it.'

Even at the height of his career as a stand-up he never lost the habit of darting around the stage. 'Nobody knew who Tommy Trinder was when I started,' he said, 'so I used to walk on and say, 'Good Evening, my name is Tommy Trinder and I'm going to sing for you – you lucky people! I was brash, cheeky and self-confident. It was purely through trying to establish in the first thirty seconds what you were going to do. Then came the latecomers and that started me off ad-libbing.'

The comedian Max Wall worked with Trinder on the halls:

'Tommy never used jokes very much, he always said funny things. He was a bit green in those days but he was brimming over with enthusiasm for the business and how he was going to make himself a star. We became pals as

Comedian Max Wall who remained a lifelong friend of Trinder's

much as you could with Tommy because he was essentially a bloke with one idea in mind and that was to get to the top.'

Variety in the thirties was filled with off-beat characters and the most notorious musical director was Sydney Kaplan. On a Monday morning, when artistes gave him their music to rehearse with the band, he would declare that the parts were 'impossible to play.' Why not get him to do a nice clean set – for a fee? If that didn't work he would try and sell the artiste leatherette covers for their music with the name of the act embossed in 'gold' on the front.

Kaplan was the world's worst audience for a comic. Trinder often worked two or three variety theatres in an evening. For a comic this could be perilous, as you never knew what gags had been cracked before you arrived. One night Trinder told one of his best gags and was met with silence. 'Here, Sydney,' he said to the smirking conductor, 'did someone crack that gag before me?' 'Yes,' shouted back Kaplan, 'Dan Leno.'

In Trinder's early career some commentators observed elements of the cockney music hall great Harry Champion (1866-1942) in Trinder's aggressive style and staccato delivery. Few comics, then or now, talked as fast as he did and much of his act centred on a masculine world with jokes or comments about sport or sex.

The more he aped and insulted his audience the more they liked it. 'People like to be insulted,' he said. 'But it's more subtle than that. People like to be noticed. They like to be put on terms of intimate back-chat with the chap in the limelight. The most important lesson of music hall is to make every member of the audience feel you're performing for them alone.'

In later years he liked to tell of the only time a heckler had bested him. 'I was on stage in a variety theatre when a man arrived late and began shuffling along the second row. I asked whether he had had trouble parking his bike and whether he had brought a note of excuse. He looked up at me and said, 'If I had known you were here, I wouldn't have come at all.' There isn't any suitable reply to that.'

The fact that Trinder was teetotal undoubtedly contributed to the sharpness and speed of his delivery onstage, although he insisted that his aversion to drink and gambling was not a matter of principle: 'I noticed on my way up in the business how some of my colleagues were on their way down largely because of the bottle and horses,' he said.

By the mid-thirties provincial audiences were soon becoming familiar with his leer and trilby hat but he was often accused by managements of being smutty or near the knuckle.

> *'I hate zip fasteners on trousers. It's like opening*
> *a double garage door to get your bike out. I said*
> *to the wife, 'Why are your ironing your bra?*
> *You've nothing to put in it.' She said, 'I iron your*
> *underpants, don't I?'*

Dame comedian and producer, Clarkson Rose, saw Trinder appearing in Jimmy Hunter's *Follies* at the Palace Pier, Brighton in 1933. 'He wasn't as polished then, but the quality was there for all to see,' he recalled. 'I was looking for a comedian for Eastbourne and, after seeing Tommy, I persuaded the managing director of the pier at Eastbourne, Teddy Taylor, to come and see Tommy with me. After watching the performance at Brighton I said to Teddy, 'Well, what do you think?' With a curl of the lip and a supercilious smirk, he said, 'Clarkie, you must be mad. This man would be no good at all – he's far too common.'

Unsurprisingly, Trinder was not booked for sedate East-bourne audiences but continued to tour and, by 1934, was earning £15 a week as a solo act. His manager and agent then was Sydney Burns, a big name among variety agents, who regarded the up and coming Trinder as a new Max Miller. There were never any contracts between them, only a handshake, and Burns remained Trinder's manager for many years.

In the early thirties Burns also spotted the young Ukrain-ian Winogradsky brothers, a dancing act, who later became better known as Lew Grade and Bernard Delfont, two of the most powerful impresarios in British light entertain-ment.

The leading theatre impresario George Black saw the young Trinder when he was playing Birmingham Hip-podrome, where gay silent film star and highly unlikely variety act, Ramon Novarro, was topping the bill prior to making his debut at the London Palladium. Black con-trolled many entertainment venues during the thirties, including the Palladium, and was credited with bringing together the Crazy Gang. Many theatre programmes of the thirties had the words 'Produced by George Black' on their covers.

Trinder got a call to meet Black at the Moss Empire offices in London. Black gave him a two year contract and over-night his wages rose from £15 to £35 a week. The first thing Trinder did was to buy a huge American Oldsmobile on hire purchase. Trinder was flash and this was his first big toy.

In September 1936 he appeared before Royalty for the first time at Balmoral Castle, during the ten month reign of Edward VIII. The Duke of York was also there, to whom eight years later, when as King George VI, Trinder was presented, he ventured to remind the King of their earlier meeting. 'You've climbed very high since then,' said the King. 'You haven't done so badly yourself, sir,' replied Trinder.

Trinder shared Moss Empire bills with many variety greats, as well as dance bands of the era, including Roy Fox, Lew Stone and Jack Hylton, about whose bill at the Kingston Empire in May 1936, the press wrote: 'Tommy Trinder who follows, is a comedian of irresistible geniality. He has a fund of good gags and stories, and also puts across a number with great success. Tommy also acts as compère throughout, to the undoubted satisfaction of the house.'

The following year he won further acclaim when he toured in the revues *Tune In* (with Larry Adler and Max Wall) and *In Town Tonight,* but his biggest break came two years later when he was brought in by Black to help Arthur Askey's sinking *Band Waggon* show at the Palladium. For Trinder it was the beginning of a unique association with the theatre that was to last an astonishing 49 years.

TRINDER AND THE GIRLS

When I was courting the wife, I used to call her the Pilgrim. Every time I took her out I made more progress. I used to take her riding at night in my car. She thought I was a surgeon. She used to say, 'Cut it out, cut it out'. She came from a nice family. Her father was a gentleman farmer. He used to milk cows with his gloves on. He was dead unlucky. He bought a prize bull for 1000 guineas, put it in a field, and it fell in love with the cow in the next field. It jumped a barbed wire fence, it didn't jump high enough – so he sold it for a tenner. What's the good of a bull with a broken leg ?

Trinder's love life was complex. He was highly sexed and loved girls of all shapes and sizes but most of all he loved high-kicking, long-legged, glamorous chorus girls. He had affairs on the road in variety and one night stands. He broke girls' hearts, slept with married women and narrowly avoided punch-ups with angry husbands.

In 1929, long before he had hit the big time, he met Violet Bailey, a dancer, whilst on tour in a concert party. Even as

a youngster, Vi was a kindly, motherly figure and quite the reverse from the usual flighty type that Trinder adored. Vi loved and genuinely admired Trinder. The couple began an affair and eventually married in 1932.

For many years they were the archetypal devoted showbiz couple – or so it seemed. They travelled everywhere, were photographed in the papers and Trinder often credited her with his early success. He lavished gifts on her – she was often photographed wearing expensive furs and jewellery – and he paid all her bills without question.

Yet as Trinder's star rose Vi became withdrawn and she began to hate the trappings of her husband's busy showbiz life.

'Vi was with Tommy for a long time,' said Max Wall. 'But as he climbed the ladder of success she couldn't keep pace with him – and he liked his girlfriends. Tommy always played the field. He was also away a lot so they drifted apart. I remember Tommy saying, in his inimitable way, 'Well, Vi's alright. I gave her a fur coat and a flat in Brighton so she'll be comfortable with her friends down there.' And to an extent he was right because she was quite a placid person, a lovely woman.'

Friends of Trinder remember Vi with affection although Billy Cotton Jnr, former Head of the BBC, recalls a different side to her:

'Vi never laughed at anything Tommy said – ever. Tommy had a lifelong ambition to get a smile out of Vi but never realised it. My father (bandleader Billy Cotton) only had to make a mildly amusing remark and she'd explode with mirth. She hated the razzamatazz of showbusiness, and I think she only warmed to my dad because he was totally without self-regard.'

Rather surprisingly, one very glamorous variety artiste that Trinder did not fall for was Joan Rhodes, the shapely strong-woman famous for bending steel bars and tearing the London Telephone Directory in two. She and Trinder appeared on bills together and in cabaret. 'I was well aware of Tommy reputation with women,' said Rhodes. 'But he was always wary of me. I think it was the strong woman image which, although it may have been a turn-on for some men, was definitely not for him.'

Strongwoman, Joan Rhodes, effortlessly lifts Trinder up in the foyer of the Savoy Hotel in London

You Lucky People!

TRINDER IN THE WAR

'Hitler started the War – we started ENSA'.

Band Waggon was a cult radio show of the thirties and starred Arthur Askey and Richard Murdoch. Originally broadcast in January 1938, it was the first radio comedy show to present its stars in situations, rather than as stand-up comics. Askey and Murdoch's anarchic humour, based around the idea that they were sharing a flat at the top of BBC Broadcasting House, quickly caught on with the public and 'Big Hearted' Arthur and 'Stinker' Murdoch soon became huge stars. It was also the first show to use catchphrases in a big way – 'Hello playmates' and 'Ay thang yew', a pronunciation which Askey had picked up from London bus conductors and which was, bizarrely, used in the nineties to sniggering erotic effect by Mike Myers in the Austin Powers movies.

Ironically, when originally casting for *Band Waggon,* co-producers Gordon Crier and Harry S Pepper had put Trinder's name forward with Askey's but as both of them were considered equally good a coin was tossed to decide which one would get the job. Heads for Trinder, tails for Askey. It came down heads but Trinder was unavailable and so Askey joined the show. Comedy buffs and radio fans can only wonder 'what if . . . ?'

Band Waggon's silly jokes, surreal events (Askey piloting a cinema organ that goes through the roof) and daft characters (Mrs Bagwash and her daughter Nausea) existed largely in the minds of listeners enabling them to take part in the act of creation, which might explain why the theatrical stage version was a flop. The stage show couldn't live up to the listener's imagination.

The Crazy Gang who appeared with Trinder at the London Palladium

The Crazy Gang consisted of three pairs of supremely gifted music hall comics: Bud Flanagan and Chesney

You Lucky People!

Allen, Jimmy Nervo and Teddy Knox, Charlie Naughton and Jimmy Gold. They were renowned on the halls for their broad, comic slapstick and much of their success, like Trinder's, depended on their spontaneity and ad-libbing. Often teamed with fellow anarchic funster 'Monsewer' Eddie Gray, the Crazy Gang revues were a fixture at the Palladium during the winter but during the summer George Black had a problem finding suitable shows for the theatre. *Band Waggon* had been touring in early 1939 and Black decided to bring it in to the Palladium, opening on 3 July. Trinder's aggressive performing and snappy energy contrasted sharply with Askey and Murdoch's twee and gentle humour – which was out of place in the vast 2,000 seater Palladium – and he clearly enjoyed veering from the *Band Waggon* scripts.

'I remember being on stage with Tommy on several occasions,' said Askey, 'and spotting the Crazy Gang watching us and Tommy shouting, 'How about this – two men doing the work of six!'

Also in the show was a young singer and dancer billed as Ernest Wise, vocalist Bruce Trent and Billy Ternant and his band who introduced a new dance sensation – the 'Boomps-a-Daisy'.

Joining them was Jack Durrant, the American comedian whose gimmick was a back-flip. In his routine he would say, 'Clark Gable – great actor, but can he do this?' and do an acrobatic somersault. 'Arthur Askey – a funny little man, but can he do this?' and repeat the trick. One evening he told Trinder that he had been booked at the Holborn Empire as soon as he had finished his Palladium spot. He asked Trinder who he could talk about on the bill there. Trinder replied, 'Caryll and Munday are topping the bill. Just say, 'Billy Caryll – can he do this?' and you'll get a big laugh. When Durrant had left for the Holborn Trinder rang Caryll and tipped him off. Caryll was a good acrobat so when Durrant said, 'Billy Caryll – a very good comedian, but can he do this?' Caryll stepped from the wings and said, 'Of course I can,' did it, and exited with the words, 'but I don't have to!'

There had been a slump in theatre-going in the summer of 1939 as people preferred to frequent pubs and hotels to discuss the threatening situation of war and even Trinder's clowning and ad-libbing failed to attract audiences for *Band Waggon.*

The outbreak of war in September brought immediate closure of theatres on government orders. Indeed, the very radio bulletin on the morning of Sunday 3 September, in which Neville Chamberlain announced the declaration of war, continued with the announcement of the closure of theatres and cinemas. This seemed to most people an excessive reaction that took no account of the need to sustain morale and within a week the ban was lifted. In the West End a six o'clock closure was enforced for a time but *Band Waggon* closed for good. It was six months before the Palladium re-opened.

On the day that war was announced Trinder had been booked to do a concert in Bridlington:

'I left London in my car and on the way, stopped for a cup of tea. A bus came along carrying about forty expectant mothers. As they climbed off the bus I looked at the conductor and said, 'Blimey! You've had a nice time!' Continuing on my journey I was listening to the car radio when I heard that war had been declared. I decided to turn

You Lucky People!

back. I reversed the car and started on my way when an air raid warning went. I saw a shelter and everybody running to it and I thought: oh yes, one has to go to a shelter. We'd been brainwashed what to do. I stopped the car and left the engine running in my haste. A warden was ushering everyone down and they were taking off their shoes and socks because there was about six inches of water on the floor of the shelter. I said, 'If I'm going to be killed, at least I'll die with dry feet'. So I stood up top. Nothing happened. I got the car and went home.'

Despite the failure of *Band Waggon* George Black regarded Trinder as one of his prize talents. He was already preparing a new escapist revue, *Top of the World*, which was due to open at the Palladium in the Autumn of 1940. Pat Kirkwood, Flanagan and Allen, and Nervo and Knox were booked as the stars but when the latter were unavailable, Black replaced them with Trinder.

Top of the World was one of Black's most expensive productions, a book show about a barrage balloon squadron (Trinder and the Crazy Gang) who end up in another world, ruled over by extraterrestrial queen Pat Kirkwood. Rehearsals began in mid-August, just as the Battle of Britain started.

The Battle of Britain began on the morning of 13 August 1940 when more than 200 German planes set off for the southern coast of England to begin Operation Eagle, the Luftwaffe's attempt to destroy the RAF in the air and on the ground. Forty-five German planes were destroyed that day for the loss of thirteen RAF aircraft. A week later the whole of Britain was declared a defence area as the skies of Kent, Sussex and Essex were filled with aerial combat.

By the beginning of September the Battle of Britain had been lost by the Germans. This was the first setback that Hitler had received during World War Two. The Blitz on British cities – nighttime raids to enhance the fear factor – was Hitler's attempt to destroy British morale. *Top of the World* opened, complete with a hail of gunfire from the Luftwaffe, to a nervous first night audience on 4 September 1940. Trinder joked on his first entrance, 'Here I am at the London Palladium, where I've always wanted my name in lights, and blimey, they've got a blackout!'

As the bombing intensified in the West End, sirens would go shortly after the first Palladium house had started. Programme notes advised audiences they could leave if they wanted to. Bud Flanagan noted that audiences were sparse. 'It was our job to entertain them until the All Clear. We were in the theatre until all hours.'

Trinder entertained the troops in WW2. He insisted on wearing 'civvies' and not a uniform. If I'm captured by the enemy I'm *entitled* to be shot'.

'We used to climb on the roof and watch the dog fights,' said Trinder. 'Half of London seemed to be in flames.' Outside the Palladium, the sky was often rose-coloured, and each vast explosion was preceded by a flash of blinding light. Every time a whistling bomb was heard people threw themselves flat on the pavement close to walls or railings. If a performance finished before the All Clear sounded the cast would sit on stage chatting with the audience or lead them in sing-songs.

Because of the habit of staying on, Trinder earned himself the record of playing the most West End theatres in one night. 'After one show George Black asked me to go down to the Hippodrome and entertain the audience who were still there. I was talking with Bud Flanagan about how many theatres it would be possible to play in one night and decided to have a go. Bud lent me a steel helmet with Police written on it and I set off in my little MG which I had to drive without lights as there was a raid on. Altogether I played 17 theatres, stopping at the stage door and asking if they wanted me to do a ten minute spot. I was hoping to do twenty but the All Clear went after the seventeenth.'

Top of the World closed after a bomb scored a direct hit on nearby Hamleys toy shop in Regent Street. At four days, it was the shortest run in the Palladium's history.

It was the people's war and no one was safe. The Anderson shelter in the back garden or the platform on a tube station were constant reminders that everyone was involved with the fighting. There were ration books and queues for food, just as there were queues for entertainment. At the Gaumont, Haymarket there were long queues for Charlie Chaplin in *The Great Dictator* and around the corner at Leicester Square, Judy Garland and Mickey Rooney were strutting their stuff in *Strike Up The Band*.

Entertainers were hugely important during the war and their work was intimately connected with the maintenance of morale among troops and civilians. They presented emotions and responses to the war with which people could identify – the stirring rhetoric of Laurence Olivier – and most popular of all, the cheeky defiance of Tommy Trinder.

> *I was at a dinner once and the speaker didn't turn up. They were desperate for someone to make a speech, so they asked me to stand in. I said, 'I can't do that, I wouldn't know what to talk about.' 'Don't worry,' said the chairman, 'you'll think of something'. So I gave a talk about sex. And it went over sensationally. Anyway, when I got home my wife asked me how the dinner went, and I told her I had to make a speech. I didn't want to shock her, so I said I talked about sailing. The next day the missus is shopping in town and bumps into our bank manager. 'What a marvellous speech your husband gave us last night,' he told her. 'It was the best I've ever heard'. 'I can't understand why,' says the wife. 'He doesn't know much about the subject. In fact, he's only done it twice. Once he was sick, and the second time his hat fell off'.*

Trinder's material was often considered too blue – even for the troops – and although there were occasional complaints from officers, there were none from the men themselves. In an entry in her wartime diary Joyce Grenfell, who appeared in several concerts with him, wrote: 'Trinder was in terrific Palladium form. Filthy but funny.'

You Lucky People!

In London, the bombing was far from over and nightly attacks continued. For many it was a lonely Christmas, with loved ones far away, killed or maimed in the war. Trinder struggled from one variety theatre to another. He spent the 1940-41 pantomime season at Manchester Opera House playing Buttons for Emile Littler and while in the city found himself in the thick of a thirteen hour raid. On the night of the bombing he was at the Midland Hotel in company with Elsie and Doris Waters, Stanley Holloway, Sir Malcolm Sargent, Anne Ziegler and Webster Booth.

Webster Booth recalled how Trinder entertained the company and hotel guests from 6.30 in the evening until dawn the next day: 'All through the night he cracked gags; he was the life and soul of the party.'

There was no let-up with the bombing the following year. On March 8 1941 in the first major raid in London for several weeks, a bomb passed through the Rialto Cinema into the famous Café de Paris in Coventry Street and exploded on the bandstand, killing 34 people, including the bandleader Snakehips Johnson. Eleven days later on the March 19 the Luftwaffe were back in even bigger numbers and left behind 750 civilian dead in the capital.

On May 12 the theatre critic James Agate noted in his diary: 'I hear that Saturday's damage is enormous, owing to the Cup Final and week ending. Scores of fires allowed to spread which could have been stopped. The Houses of Parliament hit, also the British Museum. Overheard today at the Ritz: "I'm not a snob, but I thank heaven there are plenty of common people to clear up the mess".

By the end of May 1941 the Blitz was over. 43,000 people had been killed across Britain and 1.4m made homeless.

In December 1941 Trinder opened in a new George Black revue, *Gangway*, which co-starred Bebe Daniels and Ben Lyon, Britain's favourite American husband and wife comedy team during the war. The pair had come to London in 1936 and endeared themselves to audiences by staying through the Blitz. Expensively staged by Black, *Gangway* had costumes by Royal dressmaker Norman Hartnell plus sketches by Val Guest, the screenwriter who had scripted the Will Hay classic *Oh! Mr Porter*.

Trinder was in top form in *Gangway* and on the opening night took a swipe at rival comic, the cheeky chappie himself, Max Miller: 'Here I am at the London Palladium and Max Miller's at the Finsbury Empire,' he said. 'Time marches on!' Widely regarded as one of the greatest of all stand-up comics, Max Miller had surprisingly little sense of humour off-stage. He was certainly no fan of Trinder's and quite probably resented the younger comic's mercurial rise to fame, although it is worth noting that when signing autographs he sometimes jokingly would write 'Tommy Trinder' instead of his own autograph.

When he heard of Trinder's jibe in the Palladium show he was appalled and instructed his solicitor to write a letter to Trinder demanding the deletion of what he described as 'the objectionable gag'. In reply, Trinder suggested he use a reprisal gag. Another letter arrived in which Miller asked for the exact wording of the Trinder jibe – and a reply was sent. He wrote again to ask on what date the joke was alleged to have been made and was told. 'I knew these letters were costing Miller 6/8d a time,' said Trinder. 'And he didn't like that at all.'

Later in the run he mentioned Miller's name again. A stooge in the stalls got up, carrying a brief-case, and shouted, 'I protest, I am Max Miller's solicitor.'

Max Miller on a bill in Brighton in 1952. Miller once told Max Wall: 'I'd like to tip TommyTrinder off the end of Brighton Pier.'

'Miller regarded Tommy as an upstart,' said variety producer Jack Seaton who had known both performers since his childhood. 'At the time Miller ruled the roost. He held the longest run in straight variety at the Palladium. George Black liked Tommy and the fact that Tommy could hold a book show together which Max couldn't.'

'For a long time there was a vendetta between them,' said Max Wall. 'Their style of work was similar, with a cheeky chat to the audience and the same type of rather insolent approach, placing of the foot on the footlight guard and leaning over towards the music director to 'take the audience into their confidence.' Miller resented it greatly, and the more he resented it the more Tommy provoked him, for Tommy had a brash, couldn't-care-less attitude toward life. Miller was a friend of mine and we used to get down together to Brighton to play golf and talk. When he spoke about Tommy he said he would 'throw him off the bleedin' pier.' He hated the sight of Tommy. He really did.'

During the run of *Gangway*, an unnamed member of the cast (arguably Bebe Daniels or Ben Lyon) suggested to George Black that Trinder's name should not top the bill. Trinder joked with Black that he should remove his name and he would put up his own bills – which he did, all over London. The Borough Bill Posting Company offered him 26 hoarding sites in the capital for £265 a week.

'Because it was wartime and there was a paper shortage, advertisers were using sheet iron,' said Trinder. 'It cost me more for the iron that it did for the sites.' The hoardings were handpainted and each showed a cartoon of Trinder's jaw-jutting face and his famous slogan: 'If it's laughter you're after, Trinder's the name!' There were posters in Piccadilly Circus, Leicester Square and even one in Hebrew, written by a journalist on the *Jewish Chronicle*, outside Aldgate tube station in the heart of London's Jewish East End.

Gangway, which ran for 535 performances, was the first in a succession of revues that earned Trinder the reputation of being the Palladium's resident comedian. *Best*

Bib and Tucker, which George Black built around him, followed in November 1942. The reviews were terrific. Agate wrote in his diary: 'Tommy Trinder very funny, the Cairoli Brothers superb, and Nat Jackley slithers about the stage like Walt Disney's illustrations for Stravinsky's *Sacre du Printemps*.'

High-up servicemen in the audience often bore the brunt of Trinder's ad-libs. One afternoon a rear admiral walked in after the show had started: 'You're late, aren't you?' said Trinder. 'Still, you're excused, you had to wait for the tide to come in.' He also mocked the American troops in England as 'over-paid, over-sexed and over here' and, asked by a pedestrian on Whitehall, 'which side is the War Office on', replied, 'ours I hope.'

> *Don't look at the programme sir, the name's Trinder. The fellow doesn't believe I'm Tommy Trinder. If I'm not Tommy Trinder I'm having a hell of a time with his wife! My brother is in the Army and he applied for compassionate leave last week. The commanding officer said, 'What's wrong?' and my brother said, 'My wife's going to have a baby.' When he got his leave and he returned the CO says, 'Is it a boy or a girl?' and my brother says, 'Don't be silly, it takes months!'*

Although he had a house in Brighton on the Marine Parade – dangerously close to his sparring partner Max Miller who lived in Burlington Street – when working at the Palladium he lived in Du Cane Court, a prestigious block of service flats in Balham, South London and very often arrived for a matinee still in his pyjamas. 'I figured I had to change when I reached the theatre anyway, and in those days I could park my car right outside the stage door and make a quick streak in,' he said.

On or off-stage, his ego showed no signs of letting up. The Palladium orchestra leader wore a jacket with the words T-R-I-N-D-E-R spelt across the back and Trinder had his own dressing room completely refurbished. 'It looks like a nightclub,' said George Black wryly. 'All you need is a fruit machine.' Trinder quickly had one installed. He had headed notepaper specially printed with the words Tommy Trinder c/o The London Palladium and packets of cigarettes made for him by a tobacconist in the Burlington Arcade. Embossed on the back were the words 'Stolen from Tommy Trinder'.

Best Bib and Tucker ran straight through until August 1943 clocking up 490 performances.

Earlier in the year he had been singled out in the House of Commons for criticism for not yet having worked for Entertainments National Service Association (ENSA), a criticism that ignored the fact that he had been entertaining troops at home since the outbreak of war.

ENSA was headed by the tetchy theatrical producer Basil Dean, whose unpopularity was such that one female assistant could only get through her day by sticking pins in his effigy. It was Trinder who gave ENSA its infamous sobriquets 'Every Night Something Awful' and 'Even NAFFI stands aghast'.

> *It was Christmas Day in the barracks, the soldiers went hungry to bed. They had no Christmas pudding, 'cos the sergeant had done wot they said . . .*

Part of his wartime reserved occupation agreement was for him to serve in the Home Guard in which he was an unlikely Lieutenant in charge of a gun on Clapham Common. In between runs at the Palladium he toured troops bases in the provinces – always wearing civvies – and later he did ENSA shows in North Africa, Sicily, Malta and Burma.

'No one made more cracks about ENSA than I did,' he said. 'The organisation creaked. There was too much red tape, not enough first class talent to go round. Some of the shows scraped the bottom of the barrel and some of the stars could have done more than they did. I'm afraid there were a few stars whose main interest was the publicity the tours gave them.

'I did my shows and tours in civvies. Basil Dean had me on the carpet to tell me that I must wear battledress. He said, 'If you are captured by the enemy in civilian clothes you will be shot.' I said, 'Mr Dean, If I'm captured by the enemy I'm entitled to be shot.'

On one occasion in Blackpool he did a troop show with Jack Warner (later to find fame as television's PC Dixon of Dock Green) who did an impression of Maurice Chevalier, which had a certain poignancy because France had just fallen. The band played the French national anthem, *the Marseillaise*, quietly in the background while in ringing Shakespearean tones Warner declaimed that France would rise from the ashes again. Suddenly Trinder's voice rang out from a make-shift dressing room: 'A cup of hot water in No 9, please!', a well known catchphrase in public bath houses at the time. Warner was furious.

It wasn't all laughs for TT. At one troop show in Richmond Park he entertained the first batch of POWS on their first night home in Britain. 'It was a great privilege,' he said. 'I was determined to give them my best, yet I dried up before I started. Why? Well, my act always began with the words, 'You lucky people!' Looking at those wounded and sick men, I realised what they had been through and the words stuck in my throat. The joke would have gone down well – but I couldn't say it.'

Trinder was a close friend of the celebrated plastic surgeon Sir Archibald McIndoe, whose wartime patients at East Grinstead Hospital were servicemen who had suffered appalling burns and injuries. One of McIndoe's major problems in treating these casualties was the psychological horror the men had of their own injuries. Sir Archibald suggested to Trinder that, on one Sunday a month, he bring the cast of his Palladium show to East Grinstead to perform in concert and afterwards there would be a dance where the Palladium girls could partner the injured serv- icemen. 'They had all the guts in the world, those girls,' said Trinder. 'I have seen a girl dance with a wounded serviceman, go outside and vomit, and come back to the floor and continue to dance as if her partner had been the most handsome man on earth.'

After the war Sir Archibald said that Trinder and his girls had done more to get his patients back to some kind of normal life than any medicine could have done.

***

I also sing, you know. I had my voice trained in Italy. After my voice was trained I sang in front of the King of Italy and he was so pleased he took me for a ride with him through Rome in an open carriage. There we were driving through the streets of Rome and who should we pass but Mussolini and his batman. Mussolini turned to his batman and said, 'Who's that guy riding with Trinder?'

The night before D-Day, 6 June 1944, Trinder was giving a concert to troops in Canning Town when an RSM came up to him and asked, 'Are you the announcer?' Trinder, assuming it meant compère, answered, 'Yes' and was promptly handed a sheet with detailed embarkation orders for the troop landings the following morning. Hastily handing them back, he realised he was probably the first civilian to know that the invasion was actually on.

'I was rushed to the CO, who put me on oath not to disclose a word – otherwise he said, he would have to detain me. I gave him the fullest assurance, but my mind was far from work that evening as I plodded through the show. Then I returned home and spent a restless night waiting for the heavens to fall in the way of German reprisals. The next thing I knew was my wife shaking me with a newspaper in her hand. 'Wake up Tommy!' she said. 'We've invaded France! We've landed!' 'I know, ' I said and turned over. My wife threw down the paper. 'You get on my nerves,' she said. 'You know everything.'

A week after the allies had landed, the flying V1 bombs landed in London. Nicknamed the Buzz bomb, because of the sound of the engine, the moment of terror was the sudden silence when it cut out and fell. Yet again Londoners gritted their teeth and endured the worst but the psychological mood had changed with the expected end of the war. Theatre audiences were up and George Black wanted to put on a show which echoed the triumphant spirit of the time. He commissioned bandleader Debroy Somers to compose a fitting anthem and Somers obliged with *Happy and Glorious.*

The blackout had become a dim-out and with Trinder as its mainstay, *Happy and Glorious,* became Black's most successful show ever. Trinder was on the stage solo for over an hour cracking jokes such as 'Nice suit this, cheap too. Two pounds ten for the suit, seven quid for the coupons.'

Sheila Mathews, then an up and coming musical comedy star, took over from Zoe Gail as the leading lady in the show: 'I loved Tommy but he could be very frightening. He could also be very cruel to performers. I was seventeen when I did *Happy and Glorious*, the youngest leading lady they had ever had at the Palladium and on the first night you can imagine how terrified I was. Tommy and I had several sketches to do and in one of them he started messing about. He went right away from the script and started ad-libbing. I managed to cope but when we went off Liz Welch was standing there in the wings and she tore Tommy off a strip.

'Tommy tried to make you feel small on stage but on the other hand he was so clever at picking up on anything and turning it into a gag. After he had done his opening number he would come forward and do his spot but God help anyone who came in late. He'd stop everything and ask them, 'What's your name? Where have you come from? Don't buy a programme, I'll tell you the plot' and all that sort of thing.

'I have to say, though, he could be terribly kind. I couldn't get home at night after the show because all the tube stations were shut so he would drive me back to Du Cane

Court in Balham where he lived and he arranged for me to stay with his manager and his wife in the flat above. When Tommy and I arrived, Tommy's wife, Vi, would meet us, stone-faced and her hair all in curlers. By then their marriage was very rocky and she would literally throw the dinner at him, walk out and leave us talking together.'

During the run of *Happy and Glorious* Trinder introduced the Palladium 'Oscar'. 'Have my name done on a brass plate, not a card,' he told Black. 'I'm not one of those artists who only stays a couple of weeks.' To this day, there are specially engraved brass name plates for the stars on Palladium dressing room doors.

'Tommy was then at the height of his fame,' said Sheila Mathews. 'When he arrived at the stage door each night it was an event – he was followed by footballers, bookies, girls, you name it.'

Max Wall, then in the RAF, was a visitor: 'I'd been writing my own songs for years and sometimes Tommy bought one from me. I wrote two songs for him during the war and when I went backstage at the Palladium he duly paid me, but was extremely overgenerous in his payment, knowing me to be on fifty bob a fortnight, acting corporal unpaid.'

Happy and Glorious ran from October 3 1944 until the middle of 1946, notching up a record-breaking 938 performances. Black's triumph was sadly his last for the great showman died suddenly on March 4, 1945 after an operation. Tributes poured in for the man who was known as 'the maker of the modern variety show.'

On Monday May 7 1945 the BBC informed listeners that the following Tuesday and Wednesday were to be public holidays. At 3.00pm the next day Churchill would announce the complete surrender of all German armies.

Victory Day was wet and thundery. Bunting was strung across the streets and Victory parties were underway. The Home Guard were on parade everywhere. At 3.00pm Churchill made his broadcast. Church bells pealed and in the evening there was dancing and fireworks in the streets.

The BBC Home Service broadcast *Tribute to the King* at 8.00pm, a prelude to King George VI's address to his people half and hour later. This was followed by *Victory Parade* in which a team of commentators described the bonfires and celebrations all over Britain. Richard Dimbleby was in Whitehall and Howard Marshall outside Buckingham Palace. It seemed fitting that Tommy Trinder should give a running commentary from Lambeth.

Despite the celebrations, the war was not over. Victory over Japan did not come until August 14 and rationing was even more austere as the bulk of food supplies was diverted to war ravaged Europe.

Trinder himself flew to entertain troops in the Far East and Japan but when he arrived with an ENSA show in Singapore he was unaware that his look-a-like brother Freddie, an army technician in the area, had been doing all his jokes around the garrisons. Consequently, he could only appear at several venues and so, furiously, he cut short his visit and went on to Australia where he was a huge success, not just on that trip, but on subsequent ones too.

TRINDER AT EALING

'Champagne Charlie is me name . . .'

Cinema-going was a compulsive habit for most people during the Second World War. Some three-quarters of the adult population were cinema-goers and Trinder was one of the biggest film stars of the war, a kind of cockney everyman and comic counterpart to John Mills.

His wartime stage popularity was replicated in the cinema with appearances in Ministry of Information propaganda films (*Eating Out with Tommy Trinder,* 1941) and a run of successful films made for Ealing Studios. He had already appeared in several films in the late thirties such as *Almost a Honeymoon* and *Save a Little Sunshine* (both directed by Norman Lee, 1938) but these productions straitjack-eted him into roles that most light comedians could have played, although the latter is worth watching for the dou-ble act he does with a very young Max Wall.

Ealing Studios, under the auspices of Michael Balcon, vowed 'to grasp with both hands the opportunity of putting every phase of the war on the screen' and their key wartime productions included *Went The Day Well* (directed by Cavalcanti, 1942) and Noel Coward's *In Which we Serve* (1942).

Trinder's first film in the war was *Sailors Three* (directed by Walter Forde, 1940), a genuinely funny, flag-waving farce in which he, Claude Hulbert and Michael Wilding capture a German pocket battleship. It played to full houses all over Britain although one reviewer commented that the jokes were obviously 'subject to war rationing too.' Noel Gay wrote one of the film's songs, *All Over The Place,* especially for Trinder which Trinder occasionally used as a signature tune in place of *Tiger Rag.*

Actor Gordon Jackson who appeared with Trinder in the films *The Foreman Went to France* and *Bitter Springs*. After Trinder's death in 1989 Jackson presented a BBC Radio tribute to his old friend

You Lucky People!

Trinder proved himself to be an accomplished actor and went on to play two straight roles for Ealing in *The Foreman Went to France* (directed by Charles Frend, 1942) and *The Bells Go Down* (directed by Basil Dearden, 1944). The former was based on the true life exploits of Melbourne Johns who crossed the English Channel to smuggle vital machine tools back to Blighty. Clifford Evans and Constance Cummings tackled the mission with suitable gravitas and Trinder and Gordon Jackson provided light support as soldiers. The film was well received by the public and critics, attracting wide praise for its realism and human qualities. 'Inspiring in its heroism of ordinary people and its emphasis on the best in British character', was the verdict of one Mass-Observation respondent who also described it as 'a useful documentary of the war.'

The Bells Go Down, a smoke-grimed tribute to the work of London's firemen in the Blitz, was promoted as a starring vehicle for Trinder, the promotional material for the film declaring that 'in the part of the cockney fireman, Tommy Trinder blends laughter and pathos in his own inimitable style.' Trinder was top-billed – with James Mason – and his likeable personality adds a touch of humour to the film which makes it all the more surprising that he is one of the characters killed at the end. In propaganda terms it worked as a reminder that civilians were very much in the front line in the people's war.

When the film was released Trinder was appearing at the Palladium. One evening a man arrived late at the theatre and Trinder told him from the stage, 'This isn't a cinema, you know. You can't stay and see the beginning through again. By the way, if you want to see a good film, go round the corner to the Empire, they're showing *The Bells Go*

Down.' 'No thanks, ' shouted the latecomer, 'if I'm going to see you die, I'd rather it was at the Palladium.'

Champagne Charlie (directed by Cavalcanti, 1944), a period romp from Ealing, saw him swaggering, top-hatted and well in character as the belligerent music hall star George Leybourne, a personality not unlike himself. Beautifully recreated and superbly photographed, it co-starred Stanley Holloway as The Great Vance and had Jean Kent and Betty Warner as leading ladies.

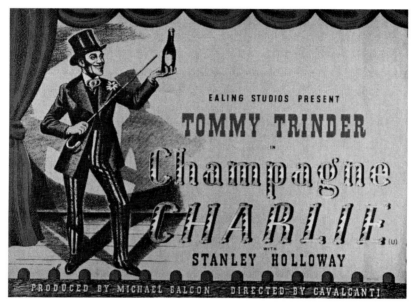

The 1944 film *Champagne Charlie* in which Trinder played music hall star Geroge Leybourne

The same year Trinder made a sequel to *Sailors Three*, the outrageous *Fiddlers Three* (directed by Harry Watt, 1944), a sort of *Roman Scandals*-cum-*Up Pompeii* littered with terrible jokes and double-entendres.

Co-starring with Trinder was sultry sex-symbol Frances Day but there were huge behind-the-scenes battles over the billing for the film. Day was billed in the same-sized letters as Trinder, but after the title, something that had never happened in her career before then.

In the film Trinder and Sonnie Hale play a couple of sailors who find themselves transported back to ancient Rome. In the opening scene the pair, cycling to Stonehenge, sing the famous Naval ditty:

Sweet Fanny Adams,
Her name tattooed on my heart
Marked on my vest
Scratched on my chest
Life would be hopeless if we had to part.
Sweet Fanny Adams,
Without her I'd be all at sea,
Fame, rank, a pile in the bank,
They mean Sweet Fanny Adams to me.

Also in the cast were Ernest Milton as Titus, a camp clothes designer, and Elisabeth Welch as a slave attendant who sings *Drums in My Heart*.

In one of the most memorable sequences, Trinder drags up as Senorita Alvarez (à la Carmen Miranda) who has arrived from Brazil to entertain the bejewelled Nero (Francis L Sullivan). Trinder parades around Nero and sings: 'My mad bolero from Uruguay/Made Emperor Nero feel very gay/He wants to go my South American way/iy iy iy iy'. A delighted Nero says: 'We are vastly impressed. We create you a Dame of the Roman Empire!'

Later the burly Sonnie Hale (who looked appalling in drag) turns up:

Nero: *Surely we have seen your face before ?*

Hale: *Oh no, imperial Caesar* (raising his voice), *excuse me, I'm a little hoarse*

Nero: *Of course. The Imperial Hunt Cup! We did you both ways!*

You Lucky People!

TRINDER IN NEW YORK

*'I don't know if you will be able to understand me.
We only invented the language – but look what
you've done to it since!'*

Val Parnell succeeded George Black as Britain's leading variety producer. He had been Black's right hand man for many years and now took over the post of managing director of Moss Empires which, among other theatres, ran the London Palladium.

Parnell was steeped in variety. His father was the ventriloquist Fred Russell and the young Val worked his way up from box office clerk at the Camberwell Empire, to booking variety acts for Vesta Tilley's husband, Sir Walter de Frece. In 1922 he became general manager of the London Palladium. He even had his own favourite seat at the theatre –number 16, row S in the stalls. 'I'm Woolworth-minded,' he said. 'I cater for the masses.'

Trinder, back from his world travels, returned to the Palladium in 1947 in *Here, There and Everywhere*, a show once again specially tailored for him. Co-starring with him were Hy Hazell and one of variety's most bizarre acts, the cod Egyptian sand dancers Wilson, Keppel and Betty. *The Stage* newspaper described the production as a 'brilliantly produced show full of meat, and when re-arranged and tightened up here and there, will be one of the best revues ever seen. Outstanding is Tommy's burlesque as Jane Russell.'

For someone so overtly heterosexual it is bizarre that Trinder had such a strong penchant for drag, best seen in his classic Carmen Miranda impersonation ('No, no, no, no, Columbus, you've discovered enough tonight!') which he had featured once in a full scale South American production sequence in *Best Bib and Tucker*, accompanied by the Edmundo Ros Orchestra, and also in the film *Fiddlers Three*. Eyelashes, in competition with the chin, were the centrepiece of the impersonation:

> Trinder: *I'll go and get my torso ready*
> Bystander: *You mean trousseau.*
> Trinder: *Don't be silly, that's always ready!*

The routines won him many fans – including drag queens.

'Tommy never enjoyed playing Dame in pantomime,' said Jack Seaton, 'but he did love dressing up as Carmen Miranda or Jane Russell. Drag queens loved him and they often used to go to the Palladium just to catch that spot. His legs were unbelievable and he could do the tummy rolls.'

He was in pantomime two years running at the Palladium, as Buttons in *Cinderella* in 1948, and the following year as Muffin in *Puss in Boots*. Evelyn Laye, who played the title role in Cinderella, made the unfortunate mistake of trying to add an extra comic line into the script whilst on stage with Trinder. Incensed, Trinder walked to the side of the stage and said, 'I see, you're the comic now, well, go ahead

You Lucky People!

and do the rest of the show then.' The audience loved it but Laye was appalled. She never forgot the incident.

Puss in Boots, The London Palladium 1949

Trinder desperately wanted to crack America, an ambition held by many British comedians but rarely achieved. In 1950 he was booked for a three week 13-minute spot as part of a floorshow at the prestigious Latin Quarter in

New York where, for the benefit of New Yorkers who had never heard of him, he was optimistically billed as 'the English Bob Hope.'

The booking made the front pages of many British newspapers with photos of him sailing from Southampton on the Queen Mary accompanied by his wife Vi. 'Since devaluation I am twice as funny as Bob Hope but at half the price,' he told one reporter.

Bob Hope - when Trinder appeared in cabaret in New York he was billed as 'The English Bob Hope'

At nighttime, the block between New York's 47th and 48th Streets had more dazzle per square inch than any other around Times Square – crowned by a neon aureole, and home to the Latin Quarter and Cotton Club.

At the Cotton Club you could see Duke Ellington, Ethel Waters, Lena Horne and Dorothy Dandrige perform in cabaret and over at the Latin Quarter Sophie Tucker and Frank Sinatra were regulars.

'Those were exciting nights', said Barbara Walters, daughter of Lou Walters who owned the Latin Quarter. 'The Latin had big, glorious shows, wonderful chorus girls, marvellous costumes. But there was no nudity. Almost always, the shows closed with a big can-can'.

You Lucky People!

Telegrams arrived for Trinder's first night from former GIs, Danny Kaye and the crew of the Queen Mary. Broadway punters put bets on whether top America comic Milton Berle – the self-styled 'thief of bad gags' – would be there to heckle. 'At the first crack from Berle, I shall bow to him and tell him that I was at the memorial service of his first film, *Always Leave Them Laughing!*' said Trinder.

Before making his entrance he was hugely nervous. 'I felt everyone watching me was armed with a machine gun,' he told one British fan. 'The butterflies in my stomach felt like seagulls.'

His act went down well and he silenced one heckler who shouted, 'To hell with England, tell us about Texas' with the line, 'Texas? We were offered that twice under the lend lease and refused it!'

Warming to the audience he said, 'You Americans are wonderful. You send all that money over to us and then you send American comedians over to take it all back again.'

Milton Berle did show up on the first night: Afterwards he quipped:'I laughed so much at Tommy Trinder's act I dropped my pencil and paper.'

The Latin Quarter's manager Eddie Davis praised Trinder's sense of timing and although back in London, several newspapers had jumped the gun and written rave articles captioned 'Trinder is the toast of Broadway!' American critics were reserved. *The New York Times* commented, 'Trinder is a pleasant, not pushing, lantern-jawed comic whose timing and sense of comedy values are not to be dismissed lightly. He errs only in that he punches a little too hard with localisms that are palpably primed for what he thinks are good local jokes, only he miscues. Cracks about the Bronx and Brooklyn must be impersonal.'

The American bible of showbiz, *Variety* liked the act and, ironically, described him as 'a sort of British Milton Berle'.

Undefeated, Trinder returned to Britain where he was already booked to appear in a lavish revue *Starlight Rendezvous*. On his arrival back in Southampton he wryly described American audiences as 'not being as friendly towards English artists as English audiences are to American.'

Throughout his career he was no stranger to appearing in London floorshows and nightclubs, often starring in late night cabaret after he had finished doing a West End show. He was also a favourite at top hotels like Grosvenor House and the Savoy.

'They say the Savoy Hotel's the comic's graveyard,' said Trinder. 'I played there twice a year. You see a dowager duchess looking at you as if to say, 'What's this?' You look back and say, 'Hello, madam. And the food's no good either, is it?' You see someone who seems to be intrigued with the act and you tell them, 'You'd better get on with your food, you can't expect them to warm it up twice.' Of course, you get complaints from managements, but who cares about that?'

At the Embassy Club he delivered one of his most famous one liners. The movie legend Orson Welles was dining in the club on the day Rita Hayworth had divorced him:

Trinder: *Trinder's the name!*
Welles: *Well, why don't you change it?*
Trinder: *Is that a proposal of marriage?*

TRINDER AND ROYALTY

'Royalty is always ready to forgive a little impertinence.'

Trinder was a favourite with Royalty often appearing at Balmoral or Windsor in private shows. King George VI was a fan and once presented him with a set of cufflinks decorated with the royal crest. On one occasion Trinder was entertaining on the lawns of Windsor Castle and every time he came to the tag of a gag he was drowned out by the sound of low flying RAF planes. Trinder turned to the King and said, 'Can't you do anything about them, Sir; after all you are the guv'nor?'

He had respect for Royalty but also gagged with and about them. 'Tommy used to come out with outrageous things,' said Max Wall. 'He had shock tactics. We were in a show in Manchester when King Edward VIII made his Abdication Speech just before he left the country. It was a very moving speech which we all listened to backstage on the radio between houses. We all felt very sad and then suddenly Tommy says, 'Well, that's that, isn't it? All he's got to do now is to go over to the South of France and work out new positions.'

A fixture in Royal Variety Performances he was often used as warm up because audiences for these shows were regarded as being difficult and reserved. In 1950 he and the Crazy Gang were the warm-ups at the Palladium and Trinder came on first waving a sheaf of newspaper cuttings. 'I'm going to read your notices from last year,' he told the audience. 'If I'd had such lousy write-ups I'd never show my face inside a theatre again.' Bud Flanagan and Teddy Knox, dressed up as charwomen, climbed into the Royal Box and

Trinder's most distinguished fan: HRH King George VI

began sweeping up. Bud threw a programme on stage and Trinder picked it up, saying: 'Blimey, it shows how often they clean this theatre. This programme is for Hengler's Circus!'

Later in his career, when he was President of the Lord's Taverners, he became friends with HRH The Duke of Edinburgh who often attended the Taverners' fund raising events. Once, however, he almost pushed his luck with HRH:

'I had to go to Buckingham Palace to talk to the Duke and Mike Parker about a cabaret,' he said. 'And I go down to see them and we sit and talk and I'm pattering away, never stopping, and the Duke of Edinburgh says, 'Look, I have some work to do, you'll have to be going.' So they take me out and I'm just going to leave when I say, 'Oh, I must tell you . . .'. And the Duke of Edinburgh says, 'Why don't you piss off?' And I say, 'That's a nice way to be shown out of Buckingham Palace.' I was speechless.'

**Trinder in charge of a charity auction on board the
RMS Queen Elizabeth, 1952**

PRINCE OF WALES

THEATRE, COVENTRY ST., W.1

(Licensed by the Lord Chamberlain)

Lessees : MOSS EMPIRES LTD.

Chairman PRINCE LITTLER   Managing Director ˙ VAL PARNELL

Artistes Booking Control	CISSIE WILLIAMS
Chief of Production Department	CHARLES HENRY
Area Supervisor . . .	E. E. BRICKNELL
Manager	GEORGE MARGRAVE
Assistant Manager .	CHARLES T. STONE
Press Representative .	JOHN A. CARLSEN

◆ ◆ ◆ ◆ ◆

◆ ◆ ◆ ◆ ◆

PRICES OF ADMISSION (including Tax)

BOX SEATS . .	. . 14/6
STALLS .	14/6, 10/6, 8/6, 6/-
CIRCLE . .	12/6, 10/6, 7/6, 5/-

BOX OFFICE (Robert F. Linsell) OPEN 10—9
ALL SEATS BOOKABLE Phone WHItehall 8681

6.15 - TWICE NIGHTLY - 8.45

VAL PARNELL
presents
THE TRINDER SHOW

"FANCY FREE"

Dances and Ensembles by JOAN DAVIS
Comedy Directed by CHARLES HENRY
Dècor and Costumes designed by ERTÉ
Artistic Direction and Lighting by ALEC SHANKS
Book by BARBARA GORDON & BASIL THOMAS
Music by PHIL PARK & PHIL GREEN
Additional Numbers by MANNING SHERWIN, MICHAEL CARR and NORMAN NEWELL
Orchestra under the direction of JACK PARNELL

In accordance with the requirements of the Lord Chamberlain—
1.—The public may leave at the end of the performance by all exit doors and such doors must at that time be open. 2.—All gangways, passages and staircases must be kept entirely free from chairs or any other obstructions. 3.—Persons shall not in any circumstances be permitted to stand or sit in any of the gangways intersecting the seating, or to sit in any of the other gangways. If standing be permitted in the gangways at the sides and rear of the seating, it shall be strictly limited to the number indicated in the notices exhibited in those positions. 4.—The safety curtain must be lowered and raised in the presence of the audience.

The Management reserves the right to refuse admission to the Theatre, and to change vary, or omit without previous notice any item of the programme*

TRINDER COLD SHOULDERED

'If the audience don't heckle me, I haven't got an act'.

Trinder greeted the dawn of drab fifties class-ridden Britain with jokes about austerity, queuing, Fulham Football Club, politicians and the pneumatically breasted TV star Sabrina. He was back at the Palladium at the beginning of the decade in a two week run of *Starlight Rendezvous,* another Val Parnell revue, in which he reprised his Carmen Miranda routine and also dragged up as Mae West.

By 1951 he was widely regarded as Britain's favourite comic. He had his own radio programme, opened fetes and judged beauty competitions. He owned a Rolls-Royce with a TT1 number plate. He was never out of the newspapers. He was stinking rich.

The same year he was top billed in a new revue, *Fancy Free*, which was tried out at the Brighton Hippodrome before opening at the Prince of Wales Theatre in London. Also in the show was Pat Kirkwood, his co-star from the ill-fated *Top of the World*, but their reunion was not a happy one. In rehearsal Trinder was touchy and disruptive:

'Tommy was in trouble on the opening night,' said Kirkwood. 'First, he was highly nervous and tightened up – unusual for him – and second, the audience failed to respond to his jokes. When we reached the finale, he stepped forward to make a speech. I wish he had not done it. Two or three in the gallery were noisy. 'Not as easy as Brighton, Tommy,' one of them yelled. Tommy had to step back and eat humble pie which was not his favourite dish. So ended the first night. As the show progressed he became unbearable to work with, was rude and insulting and altogether nasty. This was a new experience for me and not one I wished to repeat.'

Kirkwood made the same mistake as Evelyn Laye had in

Leading lady Pat Kirkwood appeared with Trinder in the film *Save A Little Sunshine* (1937) and the revue *Fancy Free* (1951)

the Palladium pantomime *Cinderella* when, at one performance, she unwisely decided to tell a funny story to Trinder during one of their duets together. She got a big laugh from the audience but Trinder was apoplectic with rage and scowled at her throughout their spot. At the finale he pulled her forward then turned to the audience and

You Lucky People!

said, 'Well, we have a new comic in the show.' Leaving Kirkwood alone on stage, he went down and sat in the stalls with his arms folded and shouted, 'So you want to be funny, eh? Well, go ahead then, be funny.' Although Kirkwood was furious she got one over Trinder. She made a short speech of thanks to the audience, then left the stage to a great round of applause – leaving Trinder still sitting in the stalls.

Trinder fell foul of fifties BBC censorship on the opening night of *Fancy Free* when, in a live broadcast of the show, he was faded out in the middle of his solo spot. A BBC official said: 'There was a cut of five seconds in the broadcast because the material in the script at that point was considered unsuitable for broadcasting.'

Trinder was unabashed and told newspapers, 'The script was passed by the Lord Chamberlain and the BBC saw it beforehand. I slipped nothing into it.'

And the joke? Trinder mentioned the growing number of nude girls appearing in London shows. 'Soon,' he quipped, 'there will be 500 nude girls on London stages – that would be a thousand pities.' The he paused, and added, 'For the ladies don't like it.'

Later he commented, 'I defend the double entendre. It's part and parcel of our music hall humour. As long as it is not indecent or ugly, or offensive, the joke with the double meaning – told in Trinder's supersonic style – is something I will keep on cracking.'

It is difficult to believe now in the 21st century that such petty censorship was once the norm both in British theatre as well as in broadcasting. Max Miller regularly fell foul of the censors and in the 1940s comedian Douglas Byng was censored by the BBC when he used the word 'Gawd' in one of his comedy songs, BBC officials feeling that it would upset religious listeners.

From 1737 the text of any play or stage show to be performed before a public audience had to be submitted to the Lord Chamberlain. The intention was that every word and action to be played out upon a stage had to have the Chamberlain's sanction in advance of a play's performance.

As well as light entertainment shows such as *Fancy Free* with their seductively dressed chorus girls, the angry young playwrights of the fifties, such as John Osborne and Arnold Wesker, alarmed the Lord Chamberlain's office. The shock of the new agitated and appalled the censors.

As late as 1958 the Lord Chamberlain's office asked for the script of John Osborne's *The Entertainer* – inspired by, but not based on, Max Miller – to be radically altered. A letter sent to the Royal Court Theatre production office insisted on the following changes:

Page 27: *alter 'pouf' (twice)*
Page 30: *alter 'shagged'*
Page 43: *omit 'rogered'*
Page 44: *omit 'I always needed a jump at the end of the day – and at the beginning too, usually.'*
The song entitled 'the old church bells won't ring tonight 'cos the vicar's got the clappers'.
Substitute 'the vicar's dropped a clanger'.

The Stage Licensing Act of 1737 was finally abolished in the Theatres Act of 1968 in the wake of the Lady Chatterley obscenity trail of 1960.

You Lucky People!

***

The comedian Sid Field was widely regarded as one of the greatest comics of his generation. He was hugely admired by his peers, not least Trinder. He cracked the West End 'overnight' in 1943 when he appeared in revue – after years of working the halls all over the country on number two dates.

All his appearances onstage were in the guise of the unique characters he had created: the spiv 'Slasher Green', the camp photographer, the cinema organist, the incompetent instrumentalist and the would-be snooker player. In 1949 he played the lovable drunk Elwood P Dowd in the hit stage comedy *Harvey*. Many said it was typecasting as Field himself was a drinker and sadly died the following year at the age of 46.

Sid Field - one of Trinder's favourite comedians. After his untimely death in 1950 Trinder compèred a star-studded tribute to him at the London Palladium

Taxation had taken up most of his

savings leaving his widow with hardly any money to bring up his three children. On June 2 1951 it seems that half of showbusiness had turned out to stage a special midnight benefit show in his memory at the London Palladium, one of the most star-studded events in the theatre's history. Val Parnell asked Trinder to compère the event.

TT opened the show, ad-libbing and wise-cracking and among those on stage that night were Danny Kaye, Laurence Olivier, Vivien Leigh, Ted Ray, Florence Desmond, Jack Buchanan (singing *Lily of Laguna*), Cicely Courtneidge (singing *Vitality*), Bud Flanagan, Ben Lyon, Peter Ustinov, Orson Wells (as a conjuror with Elizabeth Taylor as his assistant), Pat Kirkwood, Noel Coward and Judy Garland. Trinder did two spots, one impersonating Frank Sinatra and, in the second, he sang *Any Old Iron*. The show was still going strong at five o'clock in the morning.

***

After the troubled run of *Fancy Free,* Trinder toured Canada and South Africa but returned to his beloved Australia in 1952 where audiences found his egocentric cockney humour akin to their own. Earning a massive £1500 a week, he bought a block of flats in Sydney and had another source of income making commercials for sausages. 'They love me out here because, the way I speak, I sound educated,' he said.

His wife, Vi, however, did not share his enthusiasm. 'She put the kibosh on the first tour that Tommy made of Australia when they were both interviewed by the press on the airport tarmac before they flew home,' said Billy Cotton Jnr. 'Tommy rhapsodised about the country, its wonderful climate, its beautiful scenery, its marvellous audiences.

Eventually, a reporter asked Vi what was the best thing she'd seen in Australia. She said, 'This aeroplane that's going to take me back to my bulldog in Brighton.'

While in Australia Trinder made a feature film, the under-rated adventure drama, *Bitter Springs*, Ealing's attempt to humanise the pressing social problem of the relationship between Australia's white and Aboriginal populations. Trinder, playing a straight role with few gags, was top billed with Aussie legend Chips Rafferty and also appearing was his pal Gordon Jackson. Some British critics bemoaned the fact that there were few expected laughs from Trinder but C A Lejeune, writing in *The Observer*, said: 'I don't often lose my heart to a film, but I have quite lost it to this one.'

While appearing in his own variety show in Australia, he suffered an accident on stage but was quick to make comic use of it. 'Everything that you see, everything that happens to you can be used in comedy,' he said. 'I fell off the stage in Australia. So I'm giving my performance in evening dress on crutches and you can see that I've got a foot in plaster with a pad underneath it. The compère introduced me and on I walk. After a while, I find I can stand on one crutch, so, quite accidentally, I say to the compère, 'Hey, would you hold my crutch!' Note this gets a laugh and I say, 'I took a chance there. By the way, I did this the first week I was here – can you imagine? – broke my leg in Australia? That's after paying National Insurance for thirty years in England!' This gets a laugh. It's really a statement of fact and it's a thing you think of.'

He originally planned to work in Australia for six months but stayed two years. It almost proved to be his downfall.

'I had gone to Australia on the crest of a wave,' he said. 'I had become a big name in England and an even bigger one 'down under'. I was asked to do another complete tour of Australia but the bright lights of London were calling. I came back with visions of my name at the top of the bill.

Trinder sharing top billing with singer Anne Shelton in a 1958 Bernard Delfont summer season. The show was staged by Palladium producer Charles Henry

You Lucky People!

'I found out, however, I was a forgotten man. I couldn't get a West End date. The music hall moguls gave me the glad hand socially and the frozen mitt professionally. In some cases, I was cold-shouldered even socially.'

Entertainment and popular culture in Britain had changed drastically since he had been away. Old style variety shows were on the wane and in came rock and roll, skiffle, 3D films and coffee bars. Out went Donald Peers and Vera Lynn, in came Elvis and Tommy Steele. Although, as a comedian, he had always moved with the times, Trinder was clearly taken aback.

'I was amazed by what I saw,' he said. 'The invasion had been highly mechanized and scientifically planned. Some of these stars, whose records sold in millions, had no stage experience at all. Some were almost entirely created by a new breed of press agents and publicity men. I thought I knew a thing or two about publicity, but these boys opened my eyes wide.'

He toyed with the idea of giving up showbusiness and opening a pub – a hazardous occupation for a teetotaller – but Sid Burns, his longtime manager, succeeded in getting him a booking, top billed, in *Cinderella On Ice* at Earls Court. Bemused by the booking, and the fact that his legs had to be insured by Lloyds of London for £250,000, Trinder taught himself to skate. 'I brought a new gag to British ice shows,' he said. 'A tiny portable transmitter that I carried while I skated, with a microphone in my buttonhole. This way I could continue to ad-lib out on the rink.'

Earls Court was not the Palladium but it kept Trinder's name in the public eye. A summer season in Great Yarmouth followed but two of the biggest changes in his life were on the horizon.

Anne Hart (wife of Ronnie Corbett) coaxes Tommy Trinder onto the ice for skating lessons

You Lucky People!

TRINDER AND TONIE

'My wife says to me, 'Don't you ever stop talking?'
And I say, 'If I stop talking, we stop eating'.

Trinder's marriage to Vi was by now in name only. Both lived apart – she in Brighton surrounded by close non-showbiz friends – and he in Fulham enjoying the company of women, sportsmen and showbiz pals. He was still fond of her – there was a bond between them. He still sent her presents and paid all her bills, but in 1948 he was cited as co-respondent in the divorce of Barrie Stanton Wicks and his wife, Diana Elizabeth.

Around the same time he began courting Gwyn Green, a talented former ENSA dancer/pianist who went on to appear in several leading West End revues including *One, Two, Three* (1947) with Binnie and Sonnie Hale, and *Four, Five, Six* (1948) with Bobby Howes and Bill Fraser.

Gwynn, nicknamed Tonie, was the daughter of Major Gilbert Lancelyn Green of the Royal Field Artillery. Tonie's sister, Siwerids, was also a dancer/pianist and her brother, a former actor with Donald Wolfit's company, became better known as the distinguished children's author Roger Lancelyn Green, famed for his retellings of Arthurian legend. Roger's son, Richard Lancelyn Green, was the world famous memorabilia collector and bibliographer of Sir Arthur Conan Doyle.

Trinder was smitten with Tonie and the couple became inseparable. There were to be no more flings for Trinder, no more one night stands or extra marital hanky-panky. After divorcing Vi, he and Tonie were married in Sydney, Australia in 1955. 'Tommy quipped that Tonie's family were going downmarket when she married him,' said Jack Seaton. The marriage was built to last and did so until Trinder's death. They had a daughter, Jane, who became a well known dancer. Jane had two children, Emma and Louise.

As well as their initials the couple had much in common with each other. Tonie was steeped in showbusiness and loved it. She was also a keen sportswoman, being a good golfer, and held a pilot's licence. After returning from Australia the couple lived in a lavish home in Walton-on-Thames which Trinder christened Tivoli House – 'I Love It' spelt backwards and also named after the theatre circuit that he had worked so often in Australia. The property, bought originally for £32,000, boasted a garden with over a thousand rose bushes and a tennis court which led out onto the local golf course.

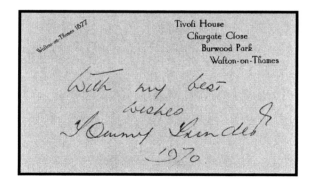

SUNDAY NIGHT AT
THE LONDON PALLADIUM

'I'll say anything!'

On Sunday September 25, 1955 at 8.00pm, three days after the newly formed ITV had begun transmission, ATV launched a variety show that would prove crucial in making the new channel an immediate success –Val Parnell's *Sunday Night at the London Palladium (SNLP)*.

Showbusiness had changed drastically during the fifties and television posed a massive threat to theatres and cinemas in Britain. Val Parnell was quick to realise the implications. When Lew Grade invited him to help form the board of one of television's first commercial channels, ATV, there is no doubt that Grade had his eye on the London Palladium, knowing that the theatre could become the very foundation on which commercial television success could be built.

Trinder was a natural choice as compère for *SNLP* and Val Parnell booked him initially for six shows.

The show would establish itself as the biggest television show of the week and Trinder's ebullient presentational style became an essential ingredient in the show's success in its early years. *SNLP* eventually topped the ratings every week for twelve years, but on the first night only 387,000 viewers tuned in since it was only available to viewers in the London area. But within weeks, as the network spread, it was watched by millions and was the subject of conversation in factories, offices and shop floors all over Britain on Monday mornings. One Church of England vicar – the Rev D P Davies of the Holy Trinity Church, Woking – started his Sunday evening service half an hour earlier so that his congregation could get home to see the show.

Parnell's formula was simple: 'I'm offering television viewers a seat in the circle at the greatest variety theatre in the world to watch the finest artists money can buy.'

Viewers had never seen anything so spectacular on television before, as the biggest names in world showbiz as well as home grown talent were brought into their living rooms in an extravaganza of music, dance and comedy.

The show, directed by Bill Lyons Shaw and Palladium associate Charles Henry, lasted an hour and opened with the high kicking Tiller Girls and then a welcome from the compère. He introduced a couple of lesser acts before launching into *Beat the Clock*, the audience participation game in which married couples (picked from the Palladium audience) played silly games which had to be completed within a set time period with a chance of winning £1,800. The second half of the show was devoted to the big name of the week and the programme was rounded off with the entire cast waving goodbye from the famous revolving stage.

The first show compèred by Trinder featured Gracie Fields and, from the USA, the popular singer Guy Mitchell. Other stars appearing during its twelve year run included Bob Hope, Judy Garland, The Beatles, Johnny Ray, The Rolling Stones and many more.

'After the first six weeks nobody said, 'Don't come anymore,' so I kept going,' said Trinder. '*SNLP* proved to me the power of television. From being a back number, I found myself as a top of the bill comedian more in demand than ever before. My years of experience in controlling an audience, ad-libbing and being able to time myself to a second stood me in good stead.'

Trinder's workload during his period as compère was punishing. During the week he was often working in a summer season or in cabaret and would be flown to the Palladium early Sunday morning by aircraft and back again early Monday. The whole of Sunday was devoted to rehearsing and transmitting the show.

Trinder started the tradition of using topical jokes, setting a pattern for subsequent compères such as Bruce Forsyth, Don Arrol, Norman Vaughan and Jim Dale to follow. On Sunday mornings he scanned newspapers for ideas and he sometimes paid a variety of scriptwriters for one-off gags.

'I reckon I read almost every daily paper published in London,' he told a *TV Mirror* reporter in 1957. 'That's where I get most of my ideas from. But I've got to take a chance on the audience knowing who or what I am talking about. I've got to risk people knowing what it means. The other day I looked back on my old scripts and found that 75 per cent of it was based on topical things and people. I simply cannot use it again. Blimey, what a waste.'

Before the show started he did a warm-up with the audience and selected suitable couples for *Beat the Clock*. One night the sound broke down and the show was delayed. Trinder went out front, sang, danced and told impromptu jokes for 90 minutes. He made headlines the next day with his introductory crack, 'Welcome to Monday morning at the London Palladium.'

Later the Arts Council of Wandsworth gave him a bronze medal for Outstanding Achievement on TV 1955-56 – holding an audience for one and a half hours. Val Parnell presented him with a gold cigarette box embossed with the words: 'To Tommy Trinder – who has abundantly proved on many occasions to be ATV's Man of the Year. From Val Parnell 1956'.

As the show was live it occasionally presented problems for Trinder. 'Luckily, I have a freak memory,' he said, 'I never write anything down. But one thing that bothered me with *SNLP* was the business of names and credits. I found it difficult to remember the name of people I introduced on *Beat the Clock*.'

In one edition of the show he had trouble with a surly lady contestant during *Beat the Clock*. She ended up winning the game and won a hairdryer. As Trinder presented it to her, she replied sulkily, 'I've already got one of those.' 'Never mind,' hissed Trinder, 'One day you might have a two-headed baby.'

Nothing, however, could have prepared him for the appearance of singer Pearl Bailey on the show in March 1957 when, after singing her opening number *I'm Tired – Tired of the Blues*, she climbed down from the stage into the orchestra pit and then over the rail into the stalls where, slurring her speech, she began chatting to the startled audience.

Her impromptu act went on for seven minutes after which she climbed back onstage with a man from the audience and began to dance with him. Palladium chiefs were aghast and brought the curtain down.

Bailey's management insisted that the star was suffering from ill-health and that she had been taking a combination of sodium amytal and cortisone for her nerves and a knee injury. The following Sunday Trinder brought the house down with his intro: 'No, please, I've got a headache,' he said. 'I wanted to take some aspirins – but after last week, I daren't.'

Long before today's comics had mastered the art of jousting with or insulting each other on television Trinder had pioneered it on *SNLP*. When the pompous American vaudeville star George Jessel gave him a card with which to announce him on the show, Trinder read it out to the audience just as it was written: 'America has sent us some great artists but here is the greatest of them all – actor, producer, writer,' and then, dragging Jessel onto the stage, added, 'and this is the man who asked me to say all this.'

Bob Hope also suffered the Trinder treatment after he insisted on having all his gags written on large cards displayed in the orchestra pit. In rehearsal Trinder gleefully did all Hope's material. 'When I went back into the wings I found Bob mopping his brow,' he said. 'He said, 'Don't you dare do that tonight.'

When the heart-throb singer Johnnie Ray appeared as star guest he told Trinder that he thought he was the funniest man he had ever seen. Trinder told him the compliment was mutual.

One star he never gagged about was the closet gay entertainer Liberace: 'It wasn't he who got upset, but his temperamental fans. One night I said, 'The Army made a man out of Liberace – and he sued them.' The next morning you couldn't see my desk for protest.'

During his run with *SNLP* Trinder claimed that Bob Monkhouse was pinching material from him and using it on his own TV shows. Monkhouse strenuously denied this but one night on *SNLP* Trinder said: 'Bob Monkhouse? There's a boy who can take a joke, and he doesn't mind whose jokes he takes.'

The press caught on to the supposed feud and Trinder refused to let it drop. The following Sunday he mentioned Monkhouse again: 'It's wrong for anyone to think I don't like Bob. I put him on a plane with Shakespeare – and nobody knows who wrote his stuff either.'

Trinder was at the height of his fame and powers as a comedian with *SNLP* and could do no wrong – or so he thought. But there was talk in showbiz circles that the Grades, Lew and Leslie, felt that he was taking over the show completely. Or asking for too much money. There was also a rumour that he was having an affair with Val Parnell's wife, Helen.

Whatever the truth, he was suddenly axed from *SNLP*. Comedian Ronnie Corbett said, 'There was some gag he did that seemed to seriously offend the Grades.' It may have been anti-semitic. Whatever it was, Trinder wasn't seen again on ITV for many years.

The all-powerful impresarios Lew Grade (left) and his brother, Bernard Delfont (right), seen here on Grade's 70th birthday. Trinder's career was damaged after a fall-out with Grade in the fifties

'Tommy was always kidding Lew Grade and I don't think Lew liked it,' said Max Wall. 'He was always referring to Lew as lying in his bed counting his money and that sort of thing. Whenever he got a chance he had a go at him. It wasn't the right thing to do.'

The Grades, Lew and Leslie, were then the most powerful men in light entertainment in Britain. Barry Cryer said: 'A falling out with them, financial or artistic, was the horse's head in the bed.'

Bruce Forsyth, then an up-and-coming young comedian, had been secretly approached to replace Trinder, although, ironically, appeared as a guest on *SNLP* just before Trinder was dropped. It was an appearance he never forgot:

'When you were the compère for a show you always worked from the prompt corner which was stage left. This meant you were near the stage manager if anything went wrong, and he could tell you what the problem was and give you instructions. I was told to come on for my spot from the right-hand side of the stage and move towards the centre where Trinder would be introducing me. So I did. But instead of Tommy going offstage the way he had come on, he walked straight into me. 'Oh,' I thought, 'have you done this on purpose?'

'I was left with no alternative but to react spontaneously – to ad-lib. I grabbed hold of him, looked him straight in the eye, spun him round, went to centre stage, looked towards where Tommy had gone, and said to the audience, 'Oooo, hasn't he got a big chin?' This got me a good laugh from the audience who probably thought it was all part of the act. But it was not. I have no way of telling if Tommy had heard the rumour that I was being considered for his job when he left but, given that it was a tradition to always walk off the same side you came on, in order to avoid bumping into the next performer, it was a very, very strange thing for him to do. I don't like to think he did it deliberately, but . . . '.

Bruce Forsyth who clashed with Trinder at the London Palladium

'It's easy to see why Tommy resented Bruce,' said Sheila Mathews. 'They were terribly alike. They both had the same chin and Bruce had the same approach to performing as Tommy. Something would happen and he would make a gag out of it.'.

Trinder's run with *SNLP* lasted from 1955 for two and a half years, with a break for another variety show, *Sunday Night at Blackpool* (ITV 1956), transmitted during the Palladium's show's summer recess. *SNLP* had kept him right at the very top of the showbiz ladder and he claimed he knew nothing of his dismissal until he read a sentence about it in *The Stage* newspaper which stated simply that Bruce Forsyth was taking over as compère. 'Nobody ever said a word. Nobody said goodbye,' he said.

He never forgot his dismissal and was quick to remind his public of it – even 20 years later when he appeared as the star guest on BBC's *The Old Boy Network*. 'There was an acid mention of the Grades when he referred to his wife telling him not to mix with certain people,' said BBC producer Michael Pointon. 'This was no doubt a passing mention of his bitter break-up with them when he considered he had been ill-treated by the organisation that had originally launched his career and benefited greatly from his special talent.'

Bruce Forsyth was an instant hit as the new compère for *SNLP* and, like Trinder, he had a natural ability for ad-libbing and audience participation. During his tenure 14m people tuned in to the show every Sunday.

His professional relationship with Trinder however, remained cool, so much so that he was alarmed to find himself appearing in a pantomime at Wimbledon in 1967 in which Trinder played Abanazar. Forsyth hastily arranged with the show's producer not to appear in any scenes with Trinder. 'The only time we appeared together was in the finale,' he said.

TRINDER AT FULHAM

'One of our players was just going to put his head in his hands and missed!'

There was never a crash or nosedive in Tommy Trinder's career. Despite his fall-out with the Grades his egocentricity and restless spirit kept him working full time throughout the fifties and sixties. 'He was married to the business,' said Max Wall. 'He worked at it just as hard in sickness as in health.'

There may not have been any more immediate Palladium dates, but for the next two decades he starred in a host of pantomimes, summer seasons and cabaret. He had one series of his own, TV show *The Trinder Box* (BBC 1959), was a regular panellist on radio's *Does The Team Think?* (BBC 1956-76) in which he pitted his wits against Ted Ray and Jimmy Edwards, and toured South Africa again. Several times he boasted to colleagues, 'I don't need the Grades to make me a star.'

His voice was beginning to sound more gravelly. Gone was the athletic poise on stage but the confidence and city street brashness were still there. The eyes were still mischievous.

As ever he updated his material – now there were gags about The Beatles, long hair, mini-skirts and the Pill – and, almost to spite the Grades, he took any job to keep him in the public eye. 'I worked for the Rank Organisation just after Tommy's falling-out with the Grades,' said Michael Pointon. 'He was doing all sorts of appearances to keep his image before the public and, when Rank were diversifying with bingo halls, he was a star guest at the opening of the re-assigned cinemas as Top Rank Bingo. He also did a cameo role in a film Val Guest made for Rank in 1964, *The Beauty Jungle*.'

'Tommy did seaside shows all over the place,' said Jack Seaton. 'I remember driving into Great Yarmouth along the Acle Straight – eight miles long and flat as a pancake either side – and getting quite a surprise. On the left side was a farm cottage with the wall split apart and Tommy, with his flair for publicity, had had the wall papered in day-glo and written in huge letters was 'I've split my sides laughing at Tommy Trinder at the Windmill Theatre.'

The Windmill Theatre, run by producer Jack Jay, was a favourite with Trinder and he returned on several occasions, often hiring a small plane which towed a banner round the resort advertising his shows.

Actor Johnny Dennis worked with him on a sixties variety bill. 'It was an afternoon concert at the Town Hall, Brixton. I was the rather young and green compère for a mixed bill. Tommy closed the bill and had the audience roaring for more. I came on for his call and he shouted over the applause, 'Oi, son, tell 'em I'm going to be late at the Savoy.' He was appearing there that night and went back to do a further ten minutes. During his act he did a few lines about Fulham Football Club. A voice from the balcony shouted, 'Fulham are rubbish!' Tommy shouted back, 'Jump!'

Trinder's love affair with Fulham FC had begun as a child when he used to sneak in and watch the game underneath a fence on the river side of the grounds. He supported the club throughout his show business career – both financially and publicly –and in 1955 was appointed chairman, making Johnny Haynes the first footballer to earn £100 a week. In 1976 he was made Life President.

There have always been close links between showbusiness and football. George Robey, once a Millwall player, frequently appeared in charity matches alongside professionals. Comedians have been some of football's most high profile supporters and Trinder paved the way for people like Eric Morecambe (a director of Luton Town) and Tommy Cannon (Chairman of Rochdale). Jimmy Tarbuck, Stan Boardman and Jasper Carrot are also examples of comics whose regional identities have been reinforced by their football allegiances.

When, as Fulham chairman, Trinder was appearing in a show at Southsea, Field Marshall Montgomery, the president of Portsmouth, heard he was in town and invited him to be his guest at Fratton Park.

After the game was over the war hero and comedian were listening to other results on the radio in the boardroom when it was announced that Fulham had won 2-0, both goals being scored by the teenage Johnny Haynes.

'That Haynes boy is going to be a great player,' enthused Trinder. 'He has a great football brain, is an excellent passer of the ball, mark my words, he'll be captain of England one day. I can say all that even though he's only eighteen years of age.'

Montgomery listened to Trinder's oration with mounting severity. 'Eighteen? What about his National Service?'

Quick as a flash, Trinder replied: 'Ah, that's the only sad thing about the lad – he's a cripple.'

At a Fulham FC board meeting Trinder once stopped the committee from having his childhood fence rebuilt so preventing youngsters from creeping in when the tide was out. And, at a West End sports dinner when a sports writer got up and said, 'The best thing about Fulham is that if the soccer's lousy you can always get a boat out at half time' Trinder retorted, 'Knowing you personally, it will be the first time you've ever pushed the boat out in your life!'

His love of Fulham was so infectious that, when it came to cracking gags about the club, even the fans joined in but he often had to apologise to the players personally. He used to joke that Fulham were 'more up and down than a bride's nightie' and that the club had got two Chinamen playing for them – 'one's called We Won Once and the other How Long Since' but in pantomime he was often likely to step out of character for a moment and tell the audience, 'didn't Fulham do well last Saturday?'

Comedian Bob Fox used to join Trinder at Craven Cottage to watch the game. 'One day I rang him to say I couldn't make it as I had a bad back. Tommy immediately quipped that 'Fulham have got two.'

No one had the last laugh over Trinder. One day he saw the words 'Trinder Out!' painted on the fences around the grounds. Under cover of night he altered the phrase

You Lucky People!

to 'Trinder Youth' thus giving him a kind of seventies street credibility.

***

Max Miller, once Trinder's arch rival, died from a heart ailment at his home in Burlington Street, Brighton on May 7 1963. In old age he would say, 'Me, Max Miller, I'm nothing. But the Cheeky Chappie will live forever.' On the day of his funeral Burlington Street was so crowded the police closed it for an hour. There were 56 floral tributes, but few from members of the entertainment profession.

Trinder told the press: 'By the death of Max Miller music hall lost one of its great personalities. He was a really terrific performer.'

Speculation was always rife in showbusiness about the relationship between the two comedians. Did Max really hate Trinder? Max Wall thought so. Jack Seaton, however, points out that both Miller and Trinder were often photographed together in the press and remembers seeing them walking along the seafront together in Brighton. Whether a real friendship existed between them or not is debatable but there can be no doubt that there was a mutual respect for each other's talent.

***

Like many variety comics in the sixties Trinder began appearing in the tough working men's clubs that had sprung up all around the country. The north dominated the circuit with giant clubs in Yorkshire and Lancashire, many of them owning their own breweries. Blue, homophobic and racist gags were the norm, bingo and girl strippers were also all part of the bill. Some variety greats such as

Max Wall, Tommy Cooper or Mrs Shufflewick (Rex Jameson) worked the clubs with relative ease and didn't have to alter their standard routines. But Trinder was far from being at home in such an atmosphere and would only play a club if the money was right.

'There's a strange thing that's happened recently,' he told writer David Nathan. 'In the days of theatre the audiences were strangers to each other. Someone would heckle and you'd come back at him and he was always the butt of your joke. The audience were on your side. But now you've got the clubs. Charlie is the club comic and Charlie heckles you and you beat him down in flames. But the audience object to this. 'That's our Charlie', they say. 'You can't do that to him'. It's a different technique now. You mustn't insult Charlie.

Ian Wright with Tommy Trinder and Ian Stewart (pianist) at the 'Baton Ball' Café de Paris, 1957

You Lucky People!

'The clubs are unbelievable. You've got no standards anymore. I worked a beautiful club once and there's a girl singer on the bill. One night I took the trouble of counting. She said seventeen bloodies, six buggers and four fucks. This is a woman! With a mixed audience. How do you follow that?'

Trinder was first and foremost a highly polished, music hall ad-lib comic who sent his audience up and he disliked personal jokes involving words such as 'Pakis' and 'queers'. He didn't swear and had never said 'fuck' on stage or off. Sixties clubland, with all its tinsel, bow ties, frilly shirts and chicken in the basket, was a far cry from the London Palladium or seaside variety. It was no place for Trinder. He got out quickly.

Like several other comedians of the period, notably Frankie Howerd and Max Wall, Trinder was taken up by the intelligentsia during the sixties. Ned Sherrin, who once described Trinder as 'the wittiest London taxi driver who never steered a cab', recruited him for his late night TV satire show *That Was The Week That Was* and he was often interviewed by the broadsheet newspapers. But, on stage or off, Trinder never compromised his approach. The ad-libs and cockney cheek were ever present.

The funniest act in showbusiness? Wilson, Betty and Keppel -
the famous cod-Egyptian eccentric sand dancing act

FELLOW COMICS

'The thing that gets me is when I hear my own ad-libs cracked by another comic. I say it's a wise crack that knows its own father.'

For much of his career Trinder enjoyed the friendship and camaraderie of sportsmen such as boxing promoter Jack Solomons and cricket legend Len Hutton as well as a host of fellow comedians. He was a longstanding member of the famous showbusiness charitable organisation The Grand Order of Water Rats whose membership included many top comics and in 1954 he was elected to the Savage Club in London where he socialised with the likes of music hall great 'Wee' Georgie Wood and *ITMA* scriptwriter Ted Kavanagh. His expression for a gathering of pros was 'Junos and Jevers' (Do you know? Did you ever?).

Max Wall was a lifelong close pal, so was Arthur Askey and Bud Flanagan. He admired the humour of northern comic Jimmy James who was renowned for his classic 'drunk' routine, although like Trinder, he too was a teetotaller. Whenever the pair appeared on a bill together Jimmy would say, 'Hello, Tom, let's get a quarter of a pound of wine gums and get stinking!'

He was close friends with Wilson, Keppel and Betty having worked with them many times on variety bills and in the 1947 Palladium revue, *Here, There and Everywhere*. Jack Wilson, an English dancer, went to America in 1909 where he met dancer Joe Keppel, and together with Betty Knox, they formed the cod-Egyptian sand dancing act which was to become famous all over the world.

On stage the two men wore loin cloths and huge head dresses that hung down to their hairy chests and both had long drooping moustaches. They shuffled about on stage, to the tune of *Ballet Egyptian*, sideways-on line making the distinctive sound of sand scraped on a board whilst Betty, dressed in silk trousers and top, was in the middle of the two. No act is more fondly remembered in variety and a rare clip of their act is the most requested piece of film ever at the British Film Institute.

'Wilson, Keppel and Betty always travelled with their own sand,' said Trinder. 'They had a big canvas bag of sand and after every show the sand would go back into it. I once travelled with them to America and when we got to New York we had to go through the customs. Have you ever tried to take a bag of sand through customs? The customs officer got them to pour it out and he said, 'Where are you taking this ?' and Joe Keppel replied, 'Las Vegas'.'

Trinder's all-time favourite comic was 'Monsewer' Eddie Gray, the moustachioed and bespectacled comedian-juggler whose patter was delivered in cockney franglais: 'Now, ce soir-that's foreign for this afternoon-moi's gonna travailler la packet of playing cards-une packet of cards, not deux,une. Now I 'ave here an ordinaire packet of playing cards-cinquante-deux in numero-fifty-two in number-ein,swine,twine,and every card parla la meme chose. I cutee in deux with vingt-six ici and vingt-six there-ci . . . '

Trinder and Gray appeared together in variety, notably in a summer show in Brighton in 1967. Gray asked Trinder to perform a sketch with him in which Trinder comes on stage and asks Gray, 'What did you have for breakfast today?' Gray replies, 'Haddock.' Trinder says, 'Finnan?' and Gray says 'No, thick 'un.'

Trinder didn't think the routine funny but agreed to rehearse it for a week. On opening night he walked on stage to a round of applause and duly asked Gray: 'What did you have for breakfast today?' 'Cornflakes,' said Gray and carried on juggling.

Gray was a notorious practical joker off-stage. His most famous prank was to peer into a letter box in a busy street and shout 'Well, how did you get in there in the first place?'

Comedian Jimmy James who, like Trinder,
was a teetotaller

TRINDER IN THE SEVENTIES

'Today the business is still a challenge. I don't want the money and I don't want the work. But I see someone and I feel, 'I can do better than that, why aren't I doing it?' I'm driving myself all the time because I feel once I let it go, I'm gone, I'm sunk.'

By the time I saw Trinder performing live in 1972 he had celebrated over 50 years in showbusiness. Logically he should have been crowned 'the grand old man of British comedy' but it was not a label he relished. He did not want to be seen as one of variety's oldest survivors, a kind of living museum piece. In 1973 he turned down an offer from producer Don Ross to appear in an 'old time' music hall show because he didn't want to be seen as an old timer.

Seventies Britain was an era culturally defined by such diverse popular entertainment as Stanley Kubrick's stark and ultra violent film *A Clockwork Orange*, the music of T-Rex, and banal, stereotyped TV comedies including *On The Buses* and *Love Thy Neighbour*. Wise-cracking Trinder, a blast from the past, but whose comedy was always fresh, seemed oddly out of place.

Yet throughout the decade, and well into the eighties, he still kept working, albeit in small seaside shows and on radio and TV nostalgia programmes. 'The last time I saw Tommy was in Newcastle, on Tyne Tees Television, and he was doing a warm-up,' said Barry Cryer. 'You could tell they had no idea who he was, this great former star. I realised that a lot of the younger members of the audience were intrigued by this quite old man with a hat. I had a drink with him afterwards. He said, 'I know what you're thinking. I just want to be part of it, that's all.'

Theatre-goer Nigel Chapman fondly recalls seeing Trinder at the Spa Pavilion, Felixstowe:

'The Spa had been costing ratepayers money for years and they threatened to stop having a summer season. TT took over the theatre on the basis that if the show didn't make money then he didn't expect to be paid. He and his wife were at the theatre most days at noon – he would wash and polish his Rolls-Royce outside the theatre – and he would mingle with the holidaymakers. He also revived the publicity stunt of having a small plane fly around the area towing a banner to advertise his show.

'My wife and I went one night to see the show and the theatre was full. TT had a routine of sticking winning tickets under the seats and the entire audience had to check under their seats to see if they had won. The first prize was ten tins of beans. The second, forty rolls of toilet paper.

'The prize I most remember was a long roll of lino. TT and the stage hands would bring the roll from backstage and present it to the unsuspecting winner who had to take it back to their seat. Not an easy task especially if you were being helped by TT. He encouraged the winner to lean the roll of lino up against the wall of the theatre – which was sloping, so the roll fell over. The next move would be for the winner to sit with the roll on their laps. TT had this routine down to an art and I will never forget the huge laughs he got that night.

'At the end of the show he got a standing ovation. People hung about thinking he would do some more gags but after a few minutes he came back on stage wearing a brown overall and carrying a roadsweeper's broom. He said to the crowd, 'Haven't you got homes to go to?' and started sweeping the stage.'

As ever he was in demand for sporting functions. 'Tommy knew a lot of people in the sporting world and could take the mickey out of them on stage,' said Jack Seaton. 'I remember one of the last big cabarets he did in London was for Arsenal Football Club. It was a dinner for the stewards and there was 200-300 people there and on the top table was the board of directors. He went along the whole of the director's line and did jokes about each one of them. He had had a look to see who was in beforehand. He would stand at the back where he couldn't be seen and he would clock who was who.'

A jazz music lover for most of his life, Trinder often compèred jazz jamborees in the sixties and seventies, big concerts in aid of the Musician's Benevolent Fund, which were staged at the giant Gaumont State Theatre in Kilburn. When he was a guest on *Desert Island Discs* back in 1951, he chose among his records music by Hoagy Carmichael, Ted Lewis, and Duke Ellington playing *Tiger Rag*.

One of Trinder's biggest admirers was the Australian writer and comic Barry Humphries ('Trinder was the first real comedian I had seen as a child') and in 1973 he asked Trinder to appear with him in his subversive and splendidly vulgar Ozzie film comedy *Barry McKenzie Holds His Own.*

A sequel to *The Adventures of Barry McKenzie* (1972), the second film, again directed by Bruce Beresford and based on Humphries' *Private Eye* comic strip, exploited Humphries' interest in Gothic tales and horror stories: When Edna Everage (Humphries) is mistaken for HM The Queen, she and her nephew Barry (Barry Crocker) are kidnapped and whisked off to Translyvania by Count Plasma (Donald Pleasance). Trinder played the ghost of Bazza's ancestor and along the way Humphries found roles for a bevy of veteran British comic talent including Roy Kinnear, 'Monsewer' Eddie Gray and Arthur English.

The climax of the film sees Edna returning to Sydney in triumph to be created a Dame by Prime Minister Gough Whitlam (played by himself in an unprecedented case of a serving Prime Minister acting himself in a Dadaist farce).

In 1974 Trinder unexpectedly returned to his favourite haunt, The London Palladium, where he compèred a variety bill, headed by Matt Monro and also featuring Max Wall. 'I didn't know who the promoter was or whether he had the money to pay me,' he said. 'It didn't matter. I'd have done it for nothing, just to get back on that stage.'

The following year he was awarded the CBE for his services to the theatre and for his charity work. The magician John Wade once suggested that the reason Trinder was only occasionally seen on television in his later years was because of the appalling state of his teeth. Trinder had a morbid fear of going to the dentist and a photograph taken of him outside Buckingham Palace on the day of his CBE investiture clearly shows several of his upper and lower teeth missing.

He did actually appear in two television programmes in the seventies. There was the nostalgia quiz show *Looks Familiar* (1974) in which he cracked gags with the veteran revue artiste Douglas Byng, with whom he had toured for ENSA. Then he was the subject of *The Old Boy Network* (1979) during which he reminisced about his career in front of an invited audience.

Cabaret artiste and female impersonator Douglas Byng who toured with Trinder in ENSA. They remained friends for many years and appeared together in TV's *Look's Familiar* in 1974

There was also the occasional pantomime. Comedy actor Jonathan Cecil recalled seeing Trinder as a larger than life Abanazar: 'Even in his seventies Trinder had this great stage presence,' said Cecil. 'He had this strong gravelly voice and you could hear every word. He was an inspiration to me as an actor.'

Sadly, the elderly Trinder was not always a box office draw although his performing stamina remained undiminished:

'I worked with him on a bill in 1976 at the Barnfield Theatre, Exeter,' said variety act, Steve Barclay. 'He was a really nice guy. But they had to paper the house and no one wanted to tell him. The press got hold of it and he was upset. I asked him to sign my banjo uke and he said, 'Well, I did the same for George Formby, so I might as well do the same for you.' He wrote, 'To Steve, with admiration from Tommy Trinder.' He insisted on doing two spots in the show and when he closed the first half he walked off the front of the stage and led the audience to the bar – where he had an orange juice.'

Still going strong in his seventies

You Lucky People!

'I saw Tommy entertaining at a tiny theatre in Sitting-bourne in the seventies,' said Michael Pointon. 'But even with a thin audience he gave them the full 'act as known', concluding on a quite moving and wistful *I Guess I'll Get the Papers and Go Home.'*

Off-stage Trinder kept in touch with old variety pals such as Max Wall and Arthur Askey and he regularly attended Sunday lodge meetings at the Grand Order of Water Rats. Such was his popularity within the organisation that he was elected King Rat three times.

But he still managed occasionally to clash with fellow pros, memorably one night when he upstaged the formidable and elderly Evelyn Laye at a Gallery First Nighter's dinner. She very decisively dismissed him from the stage, saying: 'That will do, Tommy, get off now!' It would appear that Hell hath no fury like 'Boo' Laye scorned.

No less formidable, but unlike Laye an unabashed fan, was HM The Queen Mother and in 1980 Trinder appeared before her in the 52nd *Royal Variety Show* at the London Palladium in what must have been the oldest chorus line, when thirteen artistes, including Arthur Askey, Stanley Holloway, Richard Murdoch, Chesney Allen and Trinder, with a combined age of 891 years, danced and sang their way through Flanagan and Allen's *Strollin'* .

Still making them laugh – Trinder's very last stage appearance on stage at the London Palladium just weeks before his death.
(Photo by Colin Bourner)

LAST WORDS

*'And now before I declare this meeting closed, are
there any more questions?'*

Tommy Trinder's remarkable career in comedy, a career
that had encompassed music hall, variety, films, radio,
television and international cabaret, was slowly drawing
to a close. He was still active in the 1980s, particularly
with radio programmes such as *The Trinder Box*, but his
verbal delivery was decidedly slower.

He began to suffer from heart problems and, following
a stroke in 1986, was confined to a wheelchair. In 1987
his first wife Violet Bailey died. Val Parnell had died after
a long period of ill-health in 1972 and three years later,
Trinder's bête noire, Lew Grade, wrote an autobiography
in which he only fleetingly mentioned the comedian. Grade
outlived Trinder and died in 1998.

Trinder made his final television appearance in 1989 in *I
Like The Girls Who Do* in which he recalled his contem-
porary, Max Miller.

The same year, rather bizarrely, I had a hand in his final stage appearance which, by a stroke of luck, was at the London Palladium. A BBC Radio producer had rung me to tell me that the BBC were presenting a one-off variety show at the Palladium to celebrate local radio. The show was to feature a host of variety greats including Norman Wisdom, Charlie Drake, Pearl Carr and Teddy Johnson, Eartha Kitt and many more. Was there anyone I could think of who was missing from the list ? The answer was blindingly obvious –Tommy Trinder. He had played the Palladium more times than any other comic.

'Ah, but you see Mr Trinder's in a wheelchair and we believe he's rather difficult,' said the BBC man.

'But you must ask him all the same, ' I said firmly.

'Why don't you?' said Mr BBC, passing the buck.

I got Trinder's home number from a friend and dialled. The familiar gravel voice answered. I gingerly explained the idea of the BBC show but before I could elaborate Trinder interrupted:

'Look son, it's very kind of you, but I'm retired and that's that. I'm sorry, but I'm not doing it. Tell me though, what's the name of the theatre?'

'The London Palladium,' I said.

'What time am I on?' came the reply.

TT did the show in his wheelchair and received a rapturous ovation from a Palladium full-house. Interviewed on stage about his life, he talked and wise-cracked for 20 minutes. His eyes sparkled. The laughs were big. Tommy Trinder was back where he belonged.

Trinder died a few weeks later on July 10 1989 in St Peter's Hospital, Chertsey, Surrey. He was 80. In his will he left just under £100,000. Many people expected more given his earning capacity.

In his obituaries *The Guardian* described him as 'the sharpest comedian in the business' whilst *The Independent* observed that he was 'the last of the great stars of the twice-nightly variety era. That chin, the grin, the hat, the London sparrow cockiness, and the dancing eyes were as familiar and as admired as the lions in Trafalgar Square.'

A small private family funeral was followed in March 1990 by a packed memorial service at St Bride's Church in Fleet Street, a fitting venue for a performer who had spent a lifetime making headlines. Comedians Davy Kaye and Charlie Chester gave addresses, reminding the congregation of Trinder's humour and historic ad-libs. The hymns including a rousing rendition of *Swing Low, Sweet Chariot* and the Cup Final anthem, *Abide With Me.*

As the congregation dispersed outside, a small private plane, courtesy of producer Jack Jay, flew overhead with a long banner trailing behind in the wind. On the banner, clearly printed, were the words, 'If its laughter you're after – Trinder's the name!'

FILMOGRAPHY

ALMOST A HONEYMOON (1938)

GB: 80mins

Director: Norman Lee. Screenplay: Kenneth Horne, Walter Ellis. Photography: Byron Langley. Music: John Reynders. Leading players: Tommy Trinder, Linden Travers, Wally Patch, Edmund Brown, Arthur Hambling.

AFTER DINNER (1938)

GB: 35mins

Director: Harry Pringle. Screenplay: H. Terry Wood. Music: Hastings Mann. Leading players: Tommy Trinder, Henry Lytton Jnr, George Thomas, Sylvia Welling.

SAVE A LITTLE SUNSHINE (1938)

GB: 75 mins

Director: Norman Lee. Screenplay: Vernon Clancey, Gilbert Gunn. Photography: Ernest Palmer. Music: John Reynders. Leading players: Dave Willis, Tommy Trinder, Max Wall, Pat Kirkwood, Ruth Dunning, Peggy Novak.

* Available on DVD

LAUGH IT OFF (1940)

GB: 78mins

Director: John Baxter. Screenplay: Bridget Boland, Austin Melford. Photography: James Wilson. Music: Marr Mackie, Kennedy Russell. Leading players: Tommy Trinder, Ida Barr, Wally Patch, Jean Colin, Marjorie Browne, Warren Jenkins, John Laurie.

SHE COULDN'T SAY NO (1940)

GB: 72mins

Director: Graham Cutts. Screenplay: Clifford Grey, Benjamin Kaye. Photography: Claude Friese-Greene. Music: Kenneth Leslie-Smith. Leading players: Tommy Trinder, Fred Emney, Googie Withers, Greta Gynt, Basil Radford, Wylie Watson, Cecil Parker, Doris Hare.

SAILORS THREE (1940)

Ealing: 86mins

Director: Walter Forde. Screenplay: Angus Macphail, John Dighton, Austin Melford. Photography: Gunther Krampf. Music: Ernest Irving. Leading players: Tommy Trinder, Claude Hulbert, Michael Wilding, James Hayter, John Laurie, Jeanne de Casalis, Carla Lehmann.

* Available on VHS and DVD

THE FOREMAN WENT TO FRANCE (1941)

Ealing: 87m

Director: Charles Frend. Screenplay: John Dighton, Angus Macphail, Leslie Arliss, Roger Macdougall, Diana Morgan from a story by JB Priestley. Photography: Wilkie Cooper. Music: William Walton. Leading Players: Tommy Trinder, Clifford Evans, Constance Cummings, Gordon Jackson, Robert Morley, Ernest Milton.

*Available on VHS and DVD

'Fresh, appealing comedy drama based on a true incident of World War II' (*Halliwell's Film Guide*)

WENT THE DAY WELL? (1942)

Ealing: 92mins

Director: Alberto Cavalcanti. Screenplay: Angus Mcphail, John Dighton, Diana Morgan, from a story by Graham Greene. Photography: Wilkie Cooper. Music: William Walton. Leading players: Leslie Banks, Elizabeth Allan, Frank Lawton, Basil Sydney, David Farrar, Tommy Trinder (uncredited as dance band announcer on radio).

*Available on VHS and DVD

'It has the sinister, freezing beauty of an Auden prophecy come true'. (James Agate).

THE BELLS GO DOWN (1943)

Ealing: 89mins

Director: Basil Dearden. Screenplay: Roger Macdougall, Stephen Black. Photography: Ernest Palmer. Music: Roy Douglas. Leading players: Tommy Trinder, James Mason, Finlay Currie, Mervyn Johns, Phillippa Hiatt, Phillip Friend, Meriel Forbes, Beatrice Varley, Muriel George.

You Lucky People!

* Available on VHS and DVD

'Tragi-comedy with lively scenes, a good record of the historical background of the Blitz' (*Halliwell's Film Guide*)

FIDDLERS THREE (1944)

Ealing: 87mins

Directed by Harry Watt. Screenplay: Diana Morgan, Angus Macphail. Photography: Wilkie Cooper. Music: Spike Hughes. Leading players: Tommy Trinder, Sonnie Hale, Frances Day, Francis L Sullivan, Ernest Milton, Elisabeth Welch, Mary Clare, Kay Kendall.

* Available on VHS and DVD

'Arguably the silliest film musical produced in Britain during the Second World War. Daft, but still lots of fun' (Stephen Bourne – *Brief Encounters*).

CHAMPAGNE CHARLIE (1944)

Ealing: 107 mins

Director: Alberto Cavalcanti. Screenplay: Austin Melford, Angus Macphail, John Dighton. Photography: Wilkie Cooper. Music: Ernest Irving. Leading players: Tommy Trinder, Stanley Holloway, Betty Warren, Austin Trevor, Jean Kent, Guy Middleton, Harry Fowler, James Roberston Justice.

*Available on VHS and DVD

'This period romp gave the great Tommy Trinder one of his best screen roles'. (*Radio Times Guide to Films 2007*)

BITTER SPRINGS (1949)

Ealing: 89mins

Director: Ralph Smart. Screenplay: Monja Danischewsky, W P Lipscomb. Photography: George Heath. Music: Vaughan Williams. Leading players: Chips Rafferty, Tommy Trinder, Gordon Jackson, Jean Blue, Charles Tingwell.

*Available on DVD

YOU LUCKY PEOPLE (1955)

GB: 79mins

Director: Maurice Elvey. Screenplay: Maurice Harrison, Tommy Trinder. Photography: Gordon Dines. Music: Edwin Astley. Leading players: Tommy Trinder, Dora Bryan, Mary Parker, Rolf Harris, Harold Goodwin, Michael Trubshawe, James Copeland.

MAKE MINE A MILLION (1959)

GB Elstree: 81mins

Director: Lance Comfort. Screenplay: Arthur Askey, Peter Blackmore. Photography: Arthur Grant. Music: Stanley Black. Leading players: Arthur Askey, Sid James, Dermot Walsh, Sally Barnes, Bernard Cribbins, Martin Benson, Tommy Trinder (cameo as himself).

* Available on VHS

THE BEAUTY JUNGLE (1964)

Rank/GB: 114mins

Director: Val Guest. Screenplay: Robert Muller, Val Guest. Photography: Arthur Grant. Music: Laurie Johnson. Leading players: Janette Scott, Ian Hendry, Ronald Fraser, Edmund Purdom, Tommy Trinder, Norman Bird, Francis Matthews, Janina Faye.

'Clichéd though it may seem, *The Beauty Jungle* is fascinating in its own garish way' (Hal Erickson – *All Movie Guide*).

BARRY McKENZIE HOLDS HIS OWN (1974)

Australia: 98mins

Director: Bruce Beresford. Screenplay: Barry Humphries, Bruce Beresford. Photography: Don McAlpine. Music: Peter Best. Leading players: Barry Crocker, Barry Humphries, Donald Pleasence, Dick Bentley, Tommy Trinder, Ed Devereaux, Frank Windsor, Arthur English, Roy Kinnear, John Le Mesurier.

'Splendidly vulgar and even subversive in its trouncing of racial stereotypes and political hypocrisy' (*Radio Times Guide to Films 2007*).

SELECTED RECORDINGS

TOMMY TRINDER'S PARTY (1959)

LP recorded live at the Jolly Roger Bar, Butlin's, Clacton-on-Sea.

(Fontana TFL 5073)

TOMMY TRINDER AND THE GANG (1959)

Single. *La Plume de ma Tante/On the Sunny Side of the Street.*

(Fontana H204)

YOU LUCKY PEOPLE! (1974)

LP included a medley of songs plus Trinder composition *I Can Do Without London.*

Malcolm Lockyer at the piano.

(DJM Silverline DJSL 037)

ACKNOWLEDGEMENTS

I should like to thank the following for their help with this book: Jim Arnold, Steve Barclay, Mike Carey, Nigel Chapman, Johnny Dennis, Keith Evans, Ken Fines, Eric Fowler, Bob Fox, the late Pat Kirkwood, Eric Midwinter, Billy Moore, Sheila Mathews, David Simpson, Michael Thornton, Max Tyler and John Wade. I am particularly grateful to Michael Pointon, David Drummond and Richard Anthony Baker for their encouragement and especially to Jack Seaton for the loan of assorted Tommy Trinder memorabilia.

SELECT BIBLIOGRAPHY

Askey, Arthur   *Before Your Very Eyes* (Woburn Press, 1975)

Bevan, Ian   *Top of the Bill*   (Frederick Muller, 1952)

Bourne, Stephen   *Brief Encounters* (Cassell, 1996)

Fawkes, Richard   *Fighting for a Laugh* (Macdonald and Jane's, 1978)

Fisher, John   *Funny Way to be a Hero* (Frederick Muller, 1973)

Forsyth, Bruce   *The Autobiography* (Sidgwick and Jackson, 2001)

Hepple, Peter (ed)   *That's Entertainment* (EABF Publication, 1992)

Kirkwood, Pat   *The Time of My Life* (Robert Hale, 1999)

Midwinter, Eric   *The People's Jesters* (Third Age Press, 2006)

Nathan, David   *The Laughtermakers* (Peter Owen, 1971)

Pilton, Patrick   *Every Night at The London Palladium* (Robson Books, 1976)

Rose, Clarkson   *Red Plush and Greasepaint* (Museum Press 1964)

Wall, Max   *The Fool on the Hill*   (Quartet, 1975)

INDEX

Fields, Gracie 18,78
Field, Sid 69
Flanagan and Allen
    30, 33
Flanagan, Bud 34-35
    62,70,95
Formby, George 11,104
Forsyth, Bruce 10,79,86
Fraser, Bill 75
Frece, Sir Walter de 55
Fulham Football Club
    10,16,65,75,88

Gail, Zoe 46
Garland, Judy 36,70,79
Gay, Noel 50
Gold, Jimmy 31
Grade, Lew 22,77,84,107
Gray, Eddie 31,96,102
Green, Gwyn 75
Green, Roger Lancelyn 75
Guest, Val 38,88,115

Hale, Binnie and Sonnie
    75
Hale, Sonnie 53,113
Hazell, Hy 55
Henry, Charles 78
HM The Queen Mother
    105
Holloway, Stanley 37,52
    105,113
Hope, Bob 11,58,79, 81

Howerd, Frankie 93
Howes, Bobby 75
HRH The Duke of Edin-
burgh 62/3
HRH King George VI 61/2
Hudd, Roy 9
Hulbert, Claude 50,111
Humphries, Barry 10,
    101,115
Hunter, Jimmy 21
Hutton, Len 95

Jackley, Nat 41
Jackson, Gordon 51, 71,
    112,114
Jameson, Rex 4, 92
Jay, Jack 88,109
James, Jimmy 95
Johnson, Snakehips 37
Johnson, Teddy 108
Jolson, Al 10

Kaplan, Sydney 20
Kaye, Danny 59,70
Kay, Peter 9
Kent, Jean 52,113
Kinnear, Roy 102,115
Kirkwood, Pat 10,33,
    65,70,110
Kitt, Eartha 108
Knox, Teddy (see also
Nervo and Knox) 62

If you liked *You Lucky People* ~you'll love ...

THE AMAZING MRS SHUFFLEWICK
The Life of Rex Jameson
also by Patrick Newley
£12.50 paperback + 15% postage
120 pages
ISBN 1898576 21 1
Illustrated with photographs and playbills

'Weak willed and easily lead', Mrs Shufflewick was a red-nosed, drunken old cockney who liked nothing better than to prop up the bar of her local while sipping large gin and tonics, Guinness, port and lemon or anything else that came to hand. She would tell outrageous stories about her private life to anyone who cared to listen and invariably, at the end of a disastrously alcoholic evening, would end up stark naked — all but her hairnet — on top of a 29 bus.

In real life Mrs Shufflewick was the glorious creation of Rex Jameson, a music hall great and one of radio and TV's most original and brilliant comics. Shy, difficult, bisexual and alcoholic, his private and public life often reached spectacular highs and appalling lows.

In this candid and incisive biography, Patrick Newley, who managed Jameson's later career, examines the life of the man who was lionised by comedians such as Bob Monkhouse, Barry Cryer, Danny La Rue and Barry Humphries. 'Rex was a comic genius,' said Roy Hudd. 'Even in his cups he was gloriously funny.'

RAVES & REVIEWS
about 'Mrs Shufflewick'

A brilliant monograph. ROGER LEWIS, The Daily Express

Deeply enjoyable. Patrick Newley has done us all a great favour by producing this admirably succinct memoir, with its rare photographs, outrageous anecdotes, transcribed routines and perceptive affection. SIMON CALLOW, The Guardian

Patrick Newley has written a smashing biography of Rex, The Amazing Mrs Shufflewick. It is a little masterpiece . ROY HUDD, Yours Magazine.

Unforgettable. This biography with all the laughter and desperation is a must for the bookshelf of every entertainment afficianado. WYN CALVIN

I read this book to find out more about the iconic Mrs Shufflewick, but I discovered the amazingly talented Rex Jameson. It's been a delightful journey. Pour a stiff one and read this book. MIKE WILKINS, Gay Times

A truly wonderful book. BARRY CRYER

I loved it! VICTOR SPINETTI

Patrick Newley has written a book which is almost as sad as it is funny and is immensely readable. JOHN WADE, Encore Magazine

Newley interweaves the text with extracts from Shuff's scripts which are so skillfully written that one can imagine how Jameson played them and get a real flavour of what meeting Mrs Shufflewick was really like. For those who saw Mrs S live, this is a wonderful reminder of that talent and a fitting tribute clearly written with great affection. TOM HOWARD, Rogues and Vagabonds

A book that is both very funny and very sad. Patrick Newley is a superb anecdotalist, who does not fail us here. RICHARD ANTHONY BAKER, The Stage

Other Third Age Press books
by Eric Midwinter

As one ^stage^ door closes . . . The story of John Wade: Jobbing Conjuror

As one stage door closes . . . is a study of the way the entertainment world has changed over the past 50 years by shifts in the social and economic fabric, as personally witnessed by John Wade, who, over that period, has successfully plied the ancient craft of magicianship in every possible show-business outlet. In the course of his personal journey, he crosses paths with a sparkling array of stars. This book contrives to look both in front of and behind the scenes – and then locates both in social context. From the dingy theatrical lodgings and dreary train journeys of the 1950s to the sumptuous environs of luxury liners and Hollywood glamour 40 years on, this show-business saga unrolls. **176 pages £12.50 + 15% postage**

Novel Approaches: a guide to the popular classic novel

Oh for a good read and an un-putdownable book! Despite the lurid blandishments of television, there are still many of us who turn, quietly, pensively, to the novel in leisure moments. This short text is aimed at such people whose interest has been kindled sufficiently to permit some extra contemplation and study.

Novel Approaches takes 35 novels that have stood the test of time and embeds them in historical and literary commentary – a combination of social background giving scientific objectivity, and the author's artistic subjectivity.

180 pages £9.50 + 15% postage

THIRD AGE PRESS

... an independent publishing company which recognizes that the period of life after full-time employment and family responsibility can be a time of fulfilment and continuing development . . . a time of regeneration

Third Age Press books are available by direct mail order from **Third Age Press, 6 Parkside Gardens London SW19 5EY** . .. or on order through book shops.

dnort@globalnet.co.uk   www.thirdagepress.co.uk
Please add 15% for UK postage or 20% for other countries.   UK Sterling cheques payable to *Third Age Press.*

 *. . is a series (by Eric Midwinter) that focuses on the   presentation of your unique life. These booklets seek to stimulate and guide your thoughts and words in what is acknowledged to be not only a process of value to future generations but also a personally beneficial exercise.*

A Voyage of Rediscovery: a guide to writing your life story
       ... is a 'sea chart' to guide your reminiscence & provide practical advice about the business of writing or recording your story.   **36 pages   £4.50**

Encore: a guide to planning a celebration of your life
An unusual and useful booklet that encourages you to think about the ways you would like to be remembered, hopefully in the distant future.   **20 pages   £2.00**

The Rhubarb People . . . Eric Midwinter's own witty and poignant story of growing up in Manchester in the 1930s. Also on tape including useful tips on writing or recording your story.
32 pages   £4.50   audio cassette   £5.00

OR all 3 booklets for only £10 + 15% postage

Also from Third Age Press . . .

On the Tip of Your Tongue: your memory in later life

by Dr H B Gibson . . . explores memory's history and examines what an 'ordinary' person can expect of their memory. He reveals the truth behind myths about memory and demonstrates how you can manage your large stock of memories and your life. Wittily illustrated by Rufus Segar. **160 pages   £7.00 + 15% postage**

&

A Little of What You Fancy Does You Good: your health in later life

'Managing an older body is like running a very old car – as the years go by you get to know its tricks and how to get the best out of it, so that you may keep it running sweetly for years and years' . . . so says Dr H B Gibson in his sensible and practical book which respects your intelligence and, above all, appreciates the need to enjoy later life. It explains the whys, hows and wherefores of exercise, diet and sex ~ discusses 'You and your doctor' and deals with some of the pitfalls and disabilities of later life. Illustrated by Rufus Segar.

256 pages   £7.00 + 15% postage

Buy both the above books
for the special price of only £10.00 + 15% postage

Defining Women
... on mature reflection

£12.50+ 15% postage

160 pages

Edited by Dianne Norton
illustrated by Mig

The 'extraordinary ordinary women' invited to contribute to this anthology rose magnificently to the occasion, delving deep into their personal experiences and laying bare their innermost feelings as they met a variety of challenges. Gwen Parrish, U3A News

How to be a Merry Widow
~ life after death for the older lady

by Mary Rogers
Illustrated by Mig
£12.50 + 15% postage
166 pages

• *If you are looking for a politically correct, objective view of how to cope with bereavement – do NOT buy this book!*
• *This is a book about coming to terms with widowhood after the shock of bereavement has begun to ease.*
• *Mary Rogers writes with candour and humour, in a deeply personal style. She manages to be funny, moving and at the same time, practical.*